GOD IN THE MIDST OF EVERY DAY

May these pages be a blessing —

Ruth Hickman

GOD IN THE MIDST OF EVERY DAY

Reflections on Life's Simple Gifts

RUTH·HACKMAN

AUGSBURG Publishing House • Minneapolis

GOD IN THE MIDST OF EVERY DAY
Reflections on Life's Simple Gifts

Copyright © 1986 Augsburg Publishing House

Scripture quotations unless otherwise noted are from the Holy Bible: New International Version. Copyright 1978 by the New York International Bible Society. Used by permission of Zondervan Bible Publishers.

Scripture quotations marked KJV are from the King James Version of the Bible.

Library of Congress Cataloging-in-Publication Data

Hackman, Ruth Y.
  GOD IN THE MIDST OF EVERY DAY.

    1. God—Omnipresence—Prayer-books and devotions—
English. I. Title.
BT132.H33   1986   242   86-7888
ISBN 0-8066-2207-5

Manufactured in the U.S.A.   APH 10-2643

                            7   8   9   0   1   2   3   4   5   6   7   8   9

To my grandchildren:
  Kim
    Lisa
      Shawn
        Rodney
          Andrew
            Joey
              Kevin
                Beth
                  Jason
                    And those who follow

Contents

Preface

Most of life is made up of ordinary days. "Super-spiritual" days don't come around that often. We live our Christian life at "A Rained-Out Picnic," "Behind the Wheel of a Car," or "Shopping Together." Looking for something better tomorrow is fine if we don't miss the best of today. With these thoughts I have tried to help us see God in the midst of every day.

This book was in the thinking stage for quite a few years. I owe thanks to Clarence Smith, our store's sales representative from Augsburg Publishing House. It was his idea. I'm grateful to Augsburg editors for encouraging letters and guidance throughout the writing of this book. Bonnie Bowman typed and retyped and read and reread. My son Joe helped pull it all together into a comfortable format. And every author should be blessed with my "problem"—a husband who was sure I could do it.

If just one page speaks to you, the effort was worth it.

Ruth Hackman
Allentown, Pennsylvania

God in Friendships

ACTS 16:15

" 'If you consider me a believer in the Lord,' she said, 'Come and stay at my house.' And she persuaded us."

A Warm Chair

1 PETER 4:9

"Offer hospitality to one another without grumbling."

ACTS 16:15

" 'If you consider me a believer in the Lord,' she said, 'Come and stay at my house.' And she persuaded us."

Do you remember when offering someone a warm chair was an exceptional "kindliness"? This gesture of hospitality originated before the days of central heat. Heat did not find its way into every nook and cranny of the house, and many fires burned out overnight. Furniture that was not in direct contact with the heat rays from the kitchen range or parlor stove remained frigid. This lack of warmth was not a matter of economics; it was a way of life.

A warm chair was definitely to be desired above a cold one. A warm chair was the chair you were sitting on, one warmed with your own body. This sacrificial overture to a guest told them you cared and were happy to have them.

Lydia, a biblical entrepreneur, was a dealer in purple cloth. After her conversion, her first response was to entertain the evangelistic team. She was determined. Her invitation was unyielding.

⚖

HAVE WE FORGOTTEN HOW TO PRESENT A WARM CHAIR, A BOWL OF HOT SOUP OR A COMFORTABLE BED?

A Guest Log or a Friendship Quilt

GENESIS 31:45-46

"So Jacob took a stone and set it up as a pillar. He said to his relatives, 'Gather some stones.' So they took stones and piled them in a heap, and they ate there by the heap."

GENESIS 31:48-49

"Laban said, 'This heap is a witness between you and me today.' That is why it was called Galeed. It was also called Mizpah, because he said, 'May the Lord keep watch between you and me when we are away from each other.' "

We had a wall in our home folks never seemed to forget. It was called the "Guest Log." On this wall our guests would sign their names and addresses. Some names were written sideways, straight across, in large letters, in tiny letters, high on the wall, or down near the baseboard. We had names on our wall from all over the country—even foreign countries. So many names were written there that we continued our "Guest Log" around the corner.

In addition to providing a conversation piece, I felt we helped those who had always suppressed the desire to write on walls. Few, if any, would recall the color scheme of our living room, but writing on our wall has been a symbol to them of their visit with us even after many years.

A "HEAP" MAY BE A GUEST LOG OR A FRIENDSHIP QUILT. IN WAYS LIKE THIS WE CAN REMEMBER ONE ANOTHER.

15

The "Second Table"

ROMANS 12:13

"Share with God's people who are in need. Practice hospitality."

Do you remember sitting at the "second table"? I don't mean another table, but the second sitting of the first table when there were more guests than spaces at the table. Waiting for the second table wasn't much fun. The women would politely argue back and forth and volunteer to eat the leftovers. The hostess rarely sat at the first table. She kept busy replenishing the dishes and seeing that everyone was well fed. Apprehensively, the lingering watched the "first table" devour the food—through all the courses. Some plates and silverware were washed to reset the "second table."

Even though the filling and gravy might be scarce, the mince pie a smaller portion, no one felt this showed a lack of hospitality. It was worth it just to be part of the fun.

The idea that you can seat only 10 at your table is a fallacy. It is better to share the "second table" with friends than not to have a dinner at all.

ፆ

HAS THE AVAILABILITY OF RESTAURANTS ROBBED US OF THE MANY BLESSINGS OF ENTERTAINING IN OUR HOMES?

GENESIS 18:5a

"Let me get you something to eat, so you can be refreshed and then go on your way."

16

Few Hours Together

3 JOHN: 13-14

"I have much to write you, but I do not want to do so with pen and ink. I hope to see you soon, and we will talk face to face."

PHILIPPIANS 1:3

"I thank my God every time I remember you."

Thirty-nine and a half hours was a short time to spend with our friends from Denver. It might have been 40 if the window in the cockpit of the plane had not broken. But as Stan quipped when they arrived, "I'd rather have them replace it on the ground than in the air."

We began by celebrating our wedding anniversaries together. In our many years of friendship we did not realize our anniversaries were only two days apart. Our families had tasted the cuisine in many cities, wherever booksellers had gathered. From seven in their family and seven in ours, we had dwindled to a table for four.

Early Sunday morning found us heading north to our church camp in the Pocono Mountains. We had enjoyed several weekends at Stan and Priscilla's condominium in the Rockies; now we would share our trailer in the Poconos. They were amazed at all the green foliage. I apologized for a Pennsylvania ski lift we passed; it must have looked like an anthill, compared to their Colorado runs.

The perfect weekend weather continued into the dawn of Monday morning. We rose early and drove them to the next stop of their journey, where we said good-bye.

ஐ

LIKE PAUL, WE CAN TELL OUR FRIENDS OFTEN THAT WE THINK ABOUT THEM.

17

Quilting for the Day

Winter was the time of the year when neighbors or friends put a quilt in a frame. Women went quilting for the day to a friend's house. In the evening the children and men came for fellowship.

I don't know if I ever graced a quilt with my stitches. For one thing I can't use a thimble, and whoever heard of quilting without a thimble? When a thimble is needed, I use a spool to push the needle through. However, the new foam spools make this difficult.

Today, one seldom hears of a home quilting party. I wonder how many friends and relatives would show up. How many of us would have time to "waste" on a day of quilting for someone else? And the evening fellowship: the kids would have basketball or football practice, dad a church council meeting, and mom the PTA. I would guess that by 3:00 P.M. the quilt in the frame would be abandoned, stretched to the same size it had been in the morning.

We glibly throw around words like *community, affirmation, fellowship,* and *relationships.* A "quilting" added flesh to these words. A kaffeeklatsch is not the same thing because it lacks sacrifice.

ટ્ટ

THE ART OF SHARING OURSELVES IS COSTLY—BUT REWARDING.

18

Good News

PROVERBS 25:25

"Like cold water to a weary soul is good news from a distant land."

W hen I was a child, we had to go to town to get our mail. Every evening the townsfolk met at the local grocery store that housed the post office. The grocer was the postmaster. Each mailbox had a combination dial to open the pigeonhole. Though the mail might be disappointing, you couldn't lose. The usual benchwarmers were there wrangling over problems far beyond the edge of town, while neighbors gathered to chat.

Mail is still important to us. We come home loaded down with bags and boxes. We could unlock the door and get rid of the load in a minute. But no, we spend the minute trying to decide how to distribute the weight, unlock the door, and grab the mail at the same time.

A typical day brings no letters from anyone close by or "from a distant land." The box contains mostly junk mail. Even though we know this in advance, we eagerly watch for the mailman.

1 THESSALONIANS 3:6

"But Timothy has just now come to us from you and has brought good news about your faith and love. He has told us that you always have pleasant memories of us and that you long to see us, just as we also long to see you."

❧

SHARING OUR LIFE WITH OTHERS IS MORE WELCOME THAN WE MAY THINK.

19

Group Therapy

2 TIMOTHY 1:16

"May the Lord show mercy to the household of Onesiphorus, because he often refreshed me and was not ashamed of my chains."

Sunday was for church and for "company." Some would call to check "if it would suit," but it was not uncommon for friends to invite themselves.

With my mother's home-canned foods in the basement, a meal could be quickly prepared without advanced notice. A menu of canned pork loin or sausage, mashed potatoes, and creamed peas or lima beans would make an acceptable feast anywhere. Tossed salad was not in vogue, but the choice of pickled foods was unlimited. There were cans of pickled beets and sour beans, corn relish, chow chow, sweet pickles, dill pickles, and spiced peaches.

Sunday visiting was like a game—you took turns. We had friends for Sunday dinner and later they invited us. A visit to our home meant you would sit around the table until two or three o'clock in the afternoon, just talking. These sessions were group therapy in its highest form. The "households" of Moyers, Detweilers, and Yoders often refreshed us, too.

ॐ

THERE IS NO FELLOWSHIP WITHOUT ACCEPTANCE.

ROMANS 15:7

"Accept one another, then, just as Christ accepted you, in order to bring praise to God."

Phone versus Letters

Did you ever tuck away a cherished phone call—hide it in a box? You may remember a phone call, but the possibility of retaining the exact words will be short-lived. It's simple to make a phone call to most any place in the world. However, with our easy access to make long-distance calls we are suppressing other forms of communication—like letter writing. Much of history would be sketchy if phone calls had been placed instead of letters written.

I have a timeworn box of letters which belonged to my Grandmother Yoder. It contains some letters of sympathy she received after my grandfather's death in 1933. There is a touching letter from their family doctor. Another is from the cashier at the local bank. The box also contains letters dated 1886 and 1889 from her single brother who had gone homesteading in Kansas, stating he had actually been living and working in five states and territories. Words of concern, sorrow, and love are written on these "scrolls."

Job had such a desire for his words to be immortalized.

ও

A Phone Call May Be "the Next Best Thing to Being There," but Written Words Keep Speaking Many Years Later.

The Demise of the Apron

ROMANS 12:10

"Be devoted to one another in brotherly love. Honor one another above yourselves."

I really don't like aprons. No one can accuse my children of being "tied to their mother's apron strings." But I was raised in an apron era. Who would have thought of doing dishes without an apron? My great aunt was known to wear three aprons—one on top of the other to keep the bottom one clean. To be in the kitchen without an apron was just not proper.

When company came on Sunday, the womenfolk would bring along their neatly folded aprons to help with the dishes. I wonder what a hostess would say today if I would arrive for a dinner, carrying my own apron. Eyebrows would surely rise when I'd ask where I could lay it.

It sounds humorous now, but it was a very thoughtful gesture. First, it showed you were planning to help with the dishes. Second, the hostess didn't need to wash, starch, dry, dampen, and iron an extra apron.

HEBREWS 10:24

"And let us consider how we may spur one another on toward love and good deeds."

WITH THE DEMISE OF THE APRON HAS GONE ONE MORE ACT OF KINDNESS—ONE WHICH I NEED TO REPLACE.

God in Nature

MATTHEW 6:26

"Look at the birds of the air; they do not
sow or reap or store away in barns, and yet
your heavenly Father feeds them. Are you
not much more valuable than they?"

The Hanging Nest

SONG OF SONGS 2:11-12

"See! The winter is past; the rains are over and gone. Flowers appear on the earth; the season of singing has come, the cooing of doves is heard in our land."

High above our neighbor's campsite a little bird was weaving a hanging nest. The oriole had chosen the very tip of a swinging branch for its residence. It seemed like a precarious place to begin housekeeping. Any kind of a wind would swing the nest like a pendulum. Nevertheless, the bird continued work throughout the Memorial Day weekend. Gradually, the nest looked less lacy and more firm.

How amazing that something so small as an oriole can bring a campground together! Campers gazed at the phenomenon and continued to check on its progress. The nest was difficult to reach—even for the builder. Surely, any kind of prey would be discouraged by the strategic location. Because of the nest's height, the bird was not bothered by us Homo sapiens, either.

How did this beautiful bird learn to "macrame"? Why does the nest hang instead of lie? Spring—or any season—is a good time to turn off the television and see what God had in mind through creation.

❧

CHRIST WAS IN TUNE WITH NATURE.

MATTHEW 6:26

"Look at the birds of the air; they do not sow or reap or store away in barns, and yet your heavenly Father feeds them. Are you not much more valuable than they?"

24

The Lord God Made Trees

GENESIS 2:9

"And the Lord God made all kinds of trees grow out of the ground—trees that were pleasing to the eye and good for food."

I can't name many trees by sight, but an oak is easy to spot by its leaves or bark. To identify a white birch, you don't need a horticulture degree. And to enjoy the many varieties of "pleasing to the eye" evergreens, one doesn't need to know each tree's name.

I do remember many trees by their connection to life. We had a huge tree in our backyard with a perfect branch for a swing. The swing of that swing was something else! The height we reached was beyond safety measures.

We had many beautiful shade trees. My grandfather polished his shoes in the shade of a tree "out back." The same tree was a great place to snap beans or husk sweet corn for supper.

I was never a great tree climber. I was too clumsy. However, our daughter Jenny could seek refuge from the world by climbing a tree, carrying a book, a pillow, and a Thermos.

There have been many fruit trees in my life: a Jonathan apple, a white oxheart cherry, a neighbor's persimmon. And I remember a pear tree under which the geese congregated.

Seldom, if ever, do I thank God for his creation of trees. How ungrateful.

ε♣

WE NEED TO ADD TREES TO OUR "GRATEFUL" PRAYER LIST. IMAGINE LIVING WITHOUT THEM!

EPHESIANS 5:20

"Always giving thanks to God the Father for everything, in the name of our Lord Jesus Christ."

A Mackerel Sky Means Rain

MATTHEW 16:2-3a

"When evening comes you say, 'It will be fair weather for the sky is red,' and in the morning, 'Today it will be stormy for the sky is red and overcast.'"

I'm the family weather prophet. When we lived on the other side of the city, the flag on the Pennsylvania Power and Light building was my weather vane. The waving of the stars and stripes in different directions, along with the temperature readings gave vital information for my weather predictions.

Snow storms are my specialty. A strong northeast wind with temperatures of 10°-15° is bound to bring snow—possibly a blizzard. It will seldom snow with a strong wind from the west.

A mackerel sky means rain. No one can argue with the sun drawing up water for rain.

When clouds begin to move fast, there is clear weather ahead.

If there is a patch of blue as big as a sheet, it's safe to hang out the wash.

MATTHEW 16:3b

"You know how to interpret the appearance of the sky, but you cannot interpret the signs of the times."

ACCORDING TO THIS VERSE, THE LORD IS NOT EASILY IMPRESSED

A Meadow of Daisies

ISAIAH 55:12

"You will go out in joy and be led forth in peace; the mountains and hills will burst into song before you, and all the trees of the field will clap their hands."

If it had not been for gas rationing. I would not remember Memorial Day, 1942. Because we couldn't travel, my boyfriend and I spent the day with another couple, down by the creek on our farm. The whole meadow was filled with daisies—looking like an outdoor greenhouse. I don't remember what happened when we plucked the petals with "he loves me, he loves me not." Who could resist the fun of stripping each flower till it came out right? If we tired of that, we could check if we liked butter with a buttercup.

Since gas was limited, we had to be resourceful. Also, our picnic lunch helped to stretch the three dollars a week my boyfriend Walter had for spending money. There was no escaping to television to watch the Phillies play ball. Shopping at the mall had not become a favorite pastime. There was no mall. Had we complained of boredom, our parents could have quickly remedied the situation—with work. Therefore, we did not allow ourselves the luxury of boredom.

❧

PSALM 118:24

"This is the day the Lord has made, let us rejoice and be glad in it."

NOT EVERY DAY PRESENTS US WITH A MEADOW OF DAISIES. HOWEVER, EACH SUNRISE BRINGS PROMISE OF ANOTHER DAY. FOR THIS WE CAN REJOICE.

Home Is for Rest

MARK 6:31

"Come with me by yourselves to a quiet place and get some rest."

We live on a quiet street. So what do we do weekends and holidays? We go to a Pocono Mountain campground where tents and trailers make it look like we are part of a giant exodus. The morning sleep I hoped for is interrupted by a fellow camper chopping wood. My husband, who rises early to go fishing, insists he doesn't want to disturb anyone. However, by the time he finds the bug spray, the fishworms in our trailer refrigerator, and a misplaced flashlight, I'm wide awake.

After the weekend we pack the leftover food and head back toward the city. The traffic is insane until we reach the city streets. They seem like paradise compared to a 14-wheeler in front of us and a 20-wheeler pushing us from behind.

When we arrive at home exhausted and see our neighbors leisurely picnicking on their lawns, we realize what a pleasant neighborhood we live in. Sometimes the best place to rest is at home.

❧

IMAGINE, BEING DENIED THE BEST PART OF A VACATION—COMING HOME. WHAT IF YOU COULD NEVER RETURN TO YOUR OWN FEATHER PILLOW?

MATTHEW 8:20

"Jesus replied, 'Foxes have holes and birds of the air have nests, but the Son of Man has no place to lay his head.'"

28

God
in
Education

"But the wisdom that comes from heaven is first of all pure; then peace loving, considerate, submissive, full of mercy and good fruit, impartial and sincere."

Still in First Grade

JOB 28:12

"Where can wisdom be found? Where does understanding dwell?"

JAMES 3:17

"But the wisdom that comes from heaven is first of all pure, then peace loving, considerate, submissive, full of mercy and good fruit, impartial and sincere."

Except for fifth grade, my education took place in a one-room schoolhouse. In the three schools I attended, there was no indoor plumbing. Water was carried in a bucket from a neighbor's well. However, at one school we had the luxury of a hand pump on the playground.

Play was an important part of our day. We had one full hour for lunch and two 15-minute recesses. Our playground equipment was scarce. I remember taking rails out of the fence to make a seesaw.

Our school life revolved around the platform. The teacher sat on the platform. The chalkboard was on the platform. We went to classes and sat on benches at the edge of the platform. The entire school library was housed in one or two small bookcases on the platform. On this elevation six inches high across the front of the room, our school day unfolded.

We had no science, foreign language, gym class, or study halls. Our studying was done when all the other grades went "up to class." We learned to read out loud and silently. On Friday, the spelling blanks revealed our true study for the week. The school bell tolled the beginning of the school day—and the end.

❧

WE HAVE MADE MUCH PROGRESS IN MODERN EDUCATION, BUT IN THE DIMENSION OF WISDOM, WE ARE STILL IN FIRST GRADE.

A "C" in Deportment

PROVERBS 6:20-22

"My son, keep your father's commands and do not forsake your mother's teaching. Bind them upon your heart forever; fasten them around your neck. When you walk, they will guide you; when you sleep they will watch over you; when you awake, they will speak to you."

I remember one report card on which I got a C in deportment. This was before the days of progress reports, and a C in deportment spelled trouble! This C did not need to be defined to my mother in abstract terms. In a progress report today, a C would come through something like this: "Although I have no real problem with Ruth in class, there are some areas where she needs some guidance. One area especially is her overactive verbal communication with her friends. This results in a perceptual problem which I'm sure can be dealt with, expecting promising results."

No, when that C showed up on my report card it meant I was misbehaving. For several days my mother refused to sign my report card. The mental anguish I suffered in those few days was enough to see that it would be my last C in deportment. My mother did not come to my defense. If my teacher gave me a C, then I deserved punishment at home, too. I breathed a sigh of relief when she finally signed it. I learned the lesson well; it was my last C in deportment.

PROVERBS 29:15

"The rod of correction imparts wisdom, but a child left to itself disgraces his mother."

੨ஒ

WHAT IF MY MOTHER HAD IGNORED THAT *C*?

Abilities Are Gifts from God

In times past, I was good in spelling. Now I embarrass myself. Sometimes my spelling is so bad, I can't even find it in the dictionary. How frustrating!

My husband and I were a team. I could spell and he worked out the mathematics. I still have some of my old spelling books to prove my earlier capabilities in this subject. I have not had a refresher course in spelling for almost 50 years. Admittedly, I work with lots of words. However, I no longer concentrate on their phonetic structure. For publication I must be sure the spelling is correct, so I depend on the dictionary too quickly.

I learned spelling via the "ing," "at," and "an" family. We had spelling every day with a weekly test on Friday. Our speller was an important book. Spelling was not left to osmosis. Our "McGuffey" grandmothers were even better spellers.

Before I give in to this geriatric symptom, I will try harder. Maybe I should write every word I misspell 10 times.

❧

OUR ABILITIES ARE GIFTS FROM GOD. ONLY AFTER THEY BEGIN TO SLIP AWAY FROM US, DO WE REALIZE HOW VALUABLE THEY ARE.

Who Am I?

1 CORINTHIANS 3:18

"Do not deceive yourselves. If any one of you thinks he is wise by the standards of this age, he should become a 'fool' so that he may become wise."

"Who am I?" is a very intellectual question these days. People are spending months—even years—trying to find out who they are. I honestly don't understand what they mean. Take me, for instance: I know I'm Ruth Hackman, wife of Walter Hackman and mother of five children. I'm five feet, four inches tall with graying hair. I know these are not the facts they are looking for. But what part of me tells me who I am?

Self-realization is the answer, they say. So what is self-realization? Knowing who you are!

While others try to figure out who they are, I keep wondering why they need to know. If they ever do find out who they are—then what? Since all of us are in a continual process of change, self-realization can be an endless project. It seems like a waste to spend a lifetime on something so nonproductive, while life passes by.

1 CORINTHIANS 3:19-20

"For the wisdom of this world is foolishness in God's sight. As it is written: 'He catches the wise in their craftiness'; and again, 'The Lord knows that the thoughts of the wise are futile.' "

❧

WE WILL NEVER GET TO THE BOTTOM OF "WHO AM I?"—EVEN THOUGH OUR WALLS ARE FULL OF DIPLOMAS.

God in Marriage and the Family

EPHESIANS 5:33

"However, each one of you also must love his wife as he loves himself, and the wife must respect her husband."

Morning Kisses

EPHESIANS 5:28

"In this same way, husbands ought to love their wives as their own bodies. He who loves his wife loves himself."

According to a study by a life-insurance company in West Germany, men who kiss their wives before leaving for work tend to live five years longer. This same survey showed they earn 20% to 25% more, have fewer accidents, and lose half as much time at work through illness.

The report I read said nothing about the women who were recipients of these morning kisses. I don't think that the men reaped all the benefits. From what other statistics tell us, women live longer, but morning kisses can't hurt as preventive "medicine." A kissless morning can make sorting socks seem like just sorting socks.

If the German study is accurate, a morning kiss is as beneficial as jogging or tennis—and much cheaper. I don't know why such a breakthrough is not common knowledge. It deserves headlines. Have you ever heard of such a small investment paying more dividends?

EPHESIANS 5:33

"However, each one of you also must love his wife as he loves himself and the wife must respect her husband."

WIVES SHARE THE RESPONSIBILITY FOR A LOVING RELATIONSHIP.

36

It's What Happens to the Marriage

GENESIS 2:18

"The Lord God said, 'It is not good for the man to be alone. I will make a helper suitable for him.' "

We don't have many tangible things to help us remember our wedding, but after the ceremony we went to the studio of a local photographer and posed for our wedding picture. I wore a blue, street-length dress. We bought extra pictures so we would have them for our children. Time proved this to be a smart idea.

One of the old sayings was, "You won't get rich 'til you wear out your wedding clothes." My mother thought we were married in the wrong phase of the moon. To add to our woes, my husband's sister was married the same year. When this happened in a family, it was supposed to take the luck away from the first couple married.

The lawn reception we planned became a garage reception because of the rain. A huge truck garage at the family stone quarry was cleaned and served the purpose well. As for the honeymoon, there wasn't any. It was wartime. Gas was rationed and used for necessities only, and this did not include a honeymoon.

MATTHEW 19:6

"So they are no longer two, but one. Therefore what God has joined together, let man not separate."

WHAT HAPPENS OR DOESN'T HAPPEN ON THE WEDDING DAY IS NOT REALLY IMPORTANT. IT'S WHAT HAPPENS TO THE MARRIAGE THAT COUNTS.

Early Risers and Night People

"Awake, my soul! Awake, harp and lyre! I will awaken the dawn."

Why early risers almost always marry night people is beyond me. How they stay married is still farther beyond. All five of my children knew better than to say "good morning" to me when they sat down for breakfast. If I had ever served breakfast with my hair combed and fully dressed, my husband would have gone into a state of shock. It takes all my energy just to get out of bed. I need another hour to get up nerve to stand in front of the mirror and comb my hair.

To save face and so my husband doesn't go to a diner for breakfast, I've come up with a solution. The night before, I fix the coffee pot all ready to plug in. The orange juice is mixed and in the refrigerator. The "early riser" can help himself if I don't make it.

For me civility is still in the embryo stage at 9:00 A.M. But from there on my day begins—progressing gradually toward my full potential. In 60 years I have learned early risers stay early risers and night people never change. To exclaim, "I will awaken the dawn," must be an invigorating experience!

❧

"The day is yours, and yours also the night; you established the sun and moon."

SINCE DAY AND NIGHT BELONG TO THE LORD, THAT MIGHT BE THE REASON SOME ENJOY MORNING AND OTHERS APPRECIATE THE NIGHT.

Stress and Pressure

PSALM 143:4

"So my spirit grows faint within me; my heart within me is dismayed."

In the home I think I handle pressure fairly well. When the children were sick, I coped with it. If a salesman came home for dinner, I got by with apples and dumplings. When a gown was needed for the spring concert, I sewed until the deadline. My taxi service could have been handled by Yellow Cab.

The business world for me is different. When women are fighting hard to get there, I'd like to tell them, "Hey, it's not that great!" A physically tired body usually brings sleep. That's more than you can say for a weary mind. To have your thoughts tumble around in your head like a clothes dryer, until the wee hours of the morning, is the "enviable" position one can do without. It is a joke now, but our forefathers seriously questioned the emotional stability of women when they learned how to type.

I read *Forbes, U.S. News,* and the *Wall Street Journal.* I don't want to rust in the kitchen. However, I never want to get too far away from it, either. Measuring a cup of flour, a cup of sugar, and a teaspoon of soda can alleviate the stress caused by deciphering a computer print-out.

🦐

PSALM 143:8

"Let the morning bring me word of your unfailing love, for I have put my trust in you."

OUR WORLD OF CHANGING ROLES HAS GIVEN BIRTH TO TWINS—"STRESS" AND "PRESSURE"—FOLLOWED BY MANY BOOKS ON HOW TO CONTROL THEM.

Birth Is Just the Beginning

GENESIS 3:16

"To the woman he said, 'I will greatly increase your pains in childbearing; with pain you will give birth to children.' "

When I was having babies, we didn't have the benefits of childbirth classes. Rose Ann was born on the stretcher before the doctor arrived. Becky was born one hour after labor began. My husband didn't know he was supposed to get my mind off my "discomfort." My first lesson in breathing came on the delivery table when the doctor told me to take short, panting breaths. Lamaze classes had not prepared either of us for this joint venture. Jenny, Joe, and Libby were born with a few whiffs of anesthesia, which I still considered natural childbirth.

Childbirth classes have their place, but birth is just the beginning! A child will not remember what happened in the first 24 hours. It is more important that parents are readily available in the first 24 months.

❧

PSALM 113:9

"He settles the barren woman in her home as a happy mother of children. Praise the Lord."

"Bonding" Is Not Accomplished in a Few Minutes. Hours, Days, Months, Years Are Required!

Shopping Together

JUDGES 20:11

"So all the men of Israel got together and united as one man against the city."

NEHEMIAH 4:6

"So we rebuilt the wall till all of it reached half its height, for the people worked with all their heart."

We always went shopping together—all seven of us. Every Friday night the whole family packed into our car and off we went to the farmer's market. Libby, our youngest, was barely five or six weeks old when she was included on our "night out." If we had left behind any one, it would have been punishment. When they left for college and came home for breaks, they still could not resist this weekly excursion. After the shopping was done and the bags of groceries were stashed in the car, there was no room for hitchhikers—not even in the trunk. It didn't take long to get the groceries into the house and put away. The kinds of candy we bought didn't always please everyone—nor the flavors of ice cream. But, all had something to satisfy their taste.

It's different now. Shopping to me has become a real chore. If I shop alone, it means lugging the groceries in and out of the car and putting them away myself. Granted, there's no one fighting over who carries the most bags or what flavor of ice cream to open first. However, shopping alone is not much fun. My husband has sensed my frustration and sometimes does my shopping for me, or we shop together.

❧

BUILDING THE WALL OF JERUSALEM WAS NOT WITHOUT PROBLEMS. WE KNOW, AS DID THE ISRAELITES, THERE IS GREAT STRENGTH IN TEAMWORK.

Scraping Apples

PSALM 37:23

"The Lord delights in the way of the man whose steps he has made firm."

PSALM 61:5

"For you have heard my vows, O God; you have given me the heritage of those who fear your name."

$\mathbf{D}$id you ever have your grandmother scrape an apple for you? Eating a scraped apple was like eating raw applesauce. The apple was cut in half. A table knife was used to scrape the apple. We ate the mushy pulp right off the tip of the knife.

Recently I was thinking of scraping an apple for my grandchildren, but I decided against it. To enjoy a scraped apple, everyone eats from the same knife. I wasn't sure that would be appreciated. Besides, I knew scraping an apple would sound pretty dull. How can a scraped apple compare with a super wristwatch that can take you back in time to the days of Mark Twain or the Roman Empire—all in one TV hour.

My husband remembers a special treat. His father, with his all-purpose pocket knife, would pare and core an apple. He sliced it deliciously thin and doled it out to waiting children.

🙚

FOR MY SAINTLY GRANDMOTHER AND MY HUSBAND'S DEVOUT FATHER, EVEN SCRAPING APPLES WAS AN INSPIRATION.

I Took Another Look

HEBREWS 13:5a

"Keep your lives free from the love of money and be content with what you have."

I bought a book on "window treatment." I didn't realize how drab my curtains and drapes looked until I began leafing through the pages. In the book, every pleat hung perfectly. All kinds of rods were utilized. The color schemes harmonized.

A discontented feeling began to emerge. I looked from the designer's work to my 13-year-old droopy drapes. I glanced from the neatly arranged bookshelves to my overcrowded ones, where scattered books lay horizontally on top of the customary vertical ones.

Before the seeds of dissatisfaction did their damage, I took another look. These were pictures of rooms in which no one seemed to be living. The stilted activities were placed there strictly for the photographs. Who would want to arrange 19 pillows on a sofa after every sitting? The white rugs, the gold tapestry, the brass, the china—enhanced by the various window treatments—were definitely not us. People live in our home—people who do not like to slip out of their shoes before they tread on white carpet.

❧

UNLESS OUR HOME EMBRACES THOSE WHO ENTER, IT IS ONLY A HOUSE.

ECCLESIASTES 4:6

"Better one handful with tranquillity than two handfuls with toil and chasing after the wind."

Not a New Theory

GENESIS 5:32

"After Noah was 500 years old, he became the father of Shem, Ham and Japheth."

I was 20 years old when Rosie was born and 35 when Libby appeared. The ages at which I had the other three children I must figure out between these points. On March 3, 1960, we were digging out of a snowfall of 15 inches. How do I know? Libby was born on March 2. The storm started early the next morning. The airport was closed, our doctor was snowbound, and my husband walked 15 blocks to the hospital.

What would we do if we couldn't associate events with the ages of our children—or with our own age? Becky was five months old when we moved to Allentown. We camped across country when Jenny was 14. She made snowballs in Yellowstone Park on her birthday—the Fourth of July. Rosie recited the Christmas Story from Luke 2 the Christmas before her third birthday. I began wearing glasses in my 30th year—the year Joe was born.

Memorization by association is not a new theory. The early patriarchs had it figured out.

❧

WE COULD HAVE BEEN BIBLICAL CHARACTERS. WE FUNCTION SO MUCH LIKE THEM.

GENESIS 8:13

"By the first day of the first month of Noah's six hundred and first year, the water had dried up from the earth."

44

Not
Lennox China

PROVERBS 24:3

"By wisdom a house is built and through understanding it is established."

O*ver the river and through the woods*
To grandmother's house we go,
The horse knows the way, to carry the sleigh
Through the white and drifted snow.

We lived in my grandparents' home. Their living room and our living room were only separated by our mutual stairway. So when Grammy had a Thanksgiving dinner or a Christmas dinner we were right there. To get to grandmother's house, we only had to cross over the grate of the pipeless heater at the bottom of the stairs.

We shared the same bathroom, the L-shaped porch, and the huge yard. If my parents were unhappy with this arrangement, I never knew it. We had a lot of fun when my cousins and aunts and uncles came to visit my grandparents. None of them lived farther than three miles from our home.

No family is immune from tension and problems. We had our allotment of sickness, death, and disappointment. Our family experienced two very sad deaths at Christmas—each a touching story of its own. But life was also compassionate in allowing happiness to be interspersed—the part of home we remember.

ॐ

PROVERBS 24:4

"Through knowledge its rooms are filled with rare and beautiful treasures."

A HOME IS BLESSED WHERE THE "BEAUTIFUL TREASURES" ARE NOT LENNOX CHINA—BUT PEOPLE.

45

Vacant Chairs

1 THESS. 4:9b-10

"You yourselves have been taught by God to love each other. And in fact, you do love all the brothers throughout Macedonia. Yet we urge you, brothers, to do so more and more."

In our family there are just two—my sister and I. At Christmas we take turns making the Christmas dinner. Setting a date to suit over 40 people is no small task. I know a mother of 12 who solved it by having a Christmas breakfast. I can understand her problem. Our immediate family now calls for a table setting of 21.

Much love has been lost and contention created over what holiday dinner to attend. I made up my mind long ago that I would not get uptight about the absence of family members at holiday dinners. I concluded that those who could come, could come. If others had previous arrangements, they should not feel guilty.

Though I have alleviated the dinner frustration, I try to pick a day that is likely to please the most. There are bonus times throughout the year when we all get together—unplanned. This makes up for the vacant chairs at Thanksgiving or Christmas.

We parents can cause unnecessary friction between our children and their spouses if we insist on thinking *our* family dinner is the most important.

1 PETER 3:8

"Finally, all of you, live in harmony with one another; be sympathetic, love as brothers, be compassionate and humble."

&

No Dinner Is That Important to Justify a Rift in the Family.

46

Give Us Each Day

LUKE 11:3

"Give us each day our daily bread."

I do not know how to buy food for two people—instead of seven. How can you cook one potato? I can't, so I add a few more, thinking I can fry the remains. The truth is, we seldom eat fried potatoes—maybe semiannually. And milk—I decide to take a gallon instead of a half, just in case the children come home. A week later Walt sees the obsolete date and pours the remainder down the drain.

I seldom made a single batch of cookies. I doubled it or tripled it. Now I should halve the recipe or not make any at all. Two heads of lettuce or three green peppers are an excess. Using a whole loaf of bread can be a challenge, even with a freezer. Two people can only enjoy just so many bread crumbs or so much stuffing.

"Give us each day our daily bread," is not very real to me because I can say it by rote.

LUKE 6:25

"Woe to you who are well fed now, for you will go hungry."

❧

NONE OF US KNOW WHEN THE WORDS IN LUKE 6:25 WILL MEAN *US*.

From Youth to Middle-Age

JOB 3:25

"What I feared has come upon me; What I dreaded has happened to me."

Going from seven people in our home to just the two of us has changed our lives in many ways. It has surely added longevity to almost everything in our house. Our bath towels seem to last forever. I'm sick of the old, white towels and faded, pink ones. The only good thing about our old sheets is they are worn so smooth they feel like silk. As for scatter rugs—with only four feet shuffling them anymore, I could still be washing them in the year 2000. Sometimes I wonder why I tantalize myself by looking at the exciting new designs in department stores.

I remember when most meals were a catastrophe—we spilled everything! Now it will be a marvel if I ever again wear out a tablecloth from washing. At the rate I'm using my dust brush, I won't need to replace it in my lifetime. A new tube of toothpaste is a happening. Since I no longer sponge feverish babies, a 23-cent bottle of alcohol refuses to evaporate.

ᶾ❧

ECCLESIASTES 3:1

"There is a time for everything, and a season for every activity under heaven."

GOING FROM YOUTH TO MIDDLE-AGE CAN BE DEPRESSING. A FEW NEW TOWELS AND SHEETS ADD A BIT OF COLOR. SIMPLE JOYS HELP MOST.

Crown of Splendor

PROVERBS 16:31

"Gray hair is a crown of splendor; it is attained by a righteous life."

Several years ago we wended our way to the Shenandoah Valley of Virginia. The occasion was the 40th reunion of my husband's high school class. Of the 66 who graduated, 35 attended the event.

It was well planned. All the graduates wore their picture from the class yearbook. A girl from the class made a huge sheet cake, decorated on top with the school as it appeared the year of their graduation. This was surrounded by the names of members of the class. Businessmen, pastors, nurses, farmers, housewives—all seemed to mingle as if 40 years had not elapsed.

It was difficult to believe we were now the older generation, but the reunion helped to clarify this fact. Men whose hair was thick and wavy on their pictures now had straight gray hair. Another "outsider" and I did some eavesdropping, as old friends met. Even after 40 years one could hear, "You haven't changed a bit," or "You still look the same." Surely they could not have meant there was no physical change, since many were already wearing their "crown of splendor."

ISAIAH 46:4

"Even to your old age and gray hairs I am he, I am he who will sustain you. I have made you and I will carry you; I will sustain you and will rescue you."

❧

THE LORD IS NOT ONLY A DIRECTOR OF YOUTH. HE ALSO SUPERVISES OUR "OLD AGE."

Her Books Were Finished

PSALM 89:48

"What man can live and not see death, or save himself from the power of the grave?"

Just as sure as we live, we die. The holiday season is no exception. On Monday, December 31, my mother died quite suddenly. She was 80 years old, but a young 80. Only a few weeks before, she was caring for a woman with arthritis. The Thursday before Christmas she found out she had a heart problem. That same day she went to Longwood Gardens, Delaware, for the Christmas display. Sunday night she went Christmas caroling with her church. Christmas Day she was with us for Christmas dinner at my sister's home. I'm sure she knew it was her last Christmas.

Mom still drove a car. Her odometer registered 135,000 miles. After suddenly losing the sight of her one eye, she no longer drove at night. She made a conscious effort to keep busy. She did not like to "just sit around." As for senility—not a trace.

As our daughter Jenny said, "Grammy Yoder was a woman with an up-to-date, organized, business mind, which with God's help she maintained to the end. Her books were finished—she closed out the year."

❧

REVELATION 2:10b

"Be faithful, even to the point of death, and I will give you the crown of life."

To Know She Was Ready to Go, Gave Us a Peaceful Feeling. We Knew She Was Receiving God's Crown of Life.

50

Generations Come and Go

PSALM 77:5

"I thought about the former days, the years of long ago."

As my sister and I sorted through my mother's things, we realized we could not save the memories of someone else. Brochures of places where our parents traveled meant nothing to us. There were old photographs of people who remained nameless to us.

However, many memories surfaced as we emptied drawer after drawer of its treasure. She had saved war ration books with some stamps still intact. My husband was thrilled with two unsharpened advertising pencils of "Book Store to Your Door"—his mobile bookstore was the forerunner of our own Hackman's Bible Book Store. Samples of stationery and billheads from my grandfather's stone quarry business were in excellent condition.

A rock which my father brought back from Poland, a diary of his three-month trip, and many photos helped us remember his voyage on a cattle boat after the war in 1946.

I recognized a 12-inch ruler immediately. It was the one my mother used on us for disciplinary action. The traditional cut-glass sugar bowl was in use to the end; it still had sugar in it. A huge thermometer, which always hung on our grandmother's kitchen wall, was about to be passed on to yet another generation.

ECCLESIASTES 1:4

"Generations come and generations go, but the earth remains forever."

ও

IT IS SAD THAT A LIFE'S COLLECTION OF 80 YEARS CAN BE DISPENSED OF IN A FEW DAYS.

51

God in Our Children

MATTHEW 19:14

"Jesus said, 'Let the little children come to me, and do not hinder them, for the kingdom of heaven belongs to such as these.' "

Skipping Stones and Dandelion Chains

MATTHEW 19:14

"Jesus said, 'Let the little children come to me, and do not hinder them, for the kingdom of heaven belongs to such as these.' "

My cousins and I had the best place in the world for skipping stones—the floor of our stone quarry. All the game required was a small pond and plenty of flat stones. There was skill in choosing the right stone. Learning to cradle it in your hand was also an art. The best player was the person who had the most skips as it skimmed across the water.

Striking flint stones was fun at night or in a dark place. Two pieces of flint stone were struck sharply together. Sparks would fly, followed by a strong smell of sulphur.

Blowing on grass, pressed between the thumbs, was another nature game. If the tension was right, a shrill whistle was heard as we blew through the hollow part of the thumbs.

Making dandelion chains with the stem of the flower was an inexpensive pastime too. The flower end was stuck into the stalk end. Another stem was interlocked into that circle and on and on—making a chain. In spring we had fun surprising friends with violets. Carefully, we pulled off each purple petal, revealing the tiny orange-hatted man with his feet in a bucket.

We must have been included when Jesus said, "such as these."

MATTHEW 19:15

"When he had placed his hands on them, he went on from there."

ᨠ

THE ENTHUSIASM OF CHILDREN IS BLESSED BY THE LORD.

Listen to the Children

MATTHEW 18:10

"See that you do not look down on one of these little ones. For I tell you that their angels in heaven always see the face of my Father in heaven."

MATTHEW 18:4-5

"Therefore, whoever humbles himself like this child is the greatest in the kingdom of heaven. And whoever welcomes a little child like this in my name welcomes me."

Our three-year-old grandson Andrew was watching the observance of Communion. Not willing to be left out, he cupped his little hands to make believe he had some bread too. Holding his imaginary piece of bread, he looked up at his mother and quipped, "Mine has honey on it!"

If we just took more time to listen to children! I'm sure the Lord, with the angels, smiles many times. Only a child would say:

"I forget what I feel so good about."

"We have a chicken. It throws eggs."

"We had steak and fruit cottontail."

"My shoes are eating my socks."

"What color is water?"

"Land of the children's pride . . . ."

"John always says he likes hamburglars."

"I'm sick. I need a lollipop to make me better."

"I wish it would be June—and then June and then June. Then we would be getting out of school, getting out of school, . . ."

❧

CHRIST'S THEOLOGY IS SO SIMPLE, IT'S HARD TO BELIEVE.

A Few Tears Were Shed

ISAIAH 54:13

"All your sons will be taught by the Lord, and great will be your children's peace."

JOSHUA 24:15b

"But as for me and my household, we will serve the Lord."

My husband was not too excited about the idea. He felt it was hard to recreate a setting. But it was Joe's birthday party and Joe's request: we were to conduct family worship the way we did when all five children were home—Rosie, Becky, Jenny, Joe, and Libby.

The grandchildren were thrilled as my husband told the drama-packed story of "Daniel in the Lion's Den." Three-month-old Andrew was so caught up in grandpop's enthusiasm, he laughed as if he understood. A well-known fact in the family is that my husband's Bible stories are never told the same way twice, but somewhere Daniel usually bellows to a lion, "Move over, Leo, I want a soft pillow for my head."

The "act-outs" were always the favorites. One person would act out a Bible story and the others would guess the character. This night was no exception—Miriam placed her brother Moses in the bulrushes, the good Samaritan showed his kindness, Samson killed a lion with his bare hands, and the lost sheep was found. After singing one of the nostalgic motion songs entitled, "I'm in right, out right, up right, down right, happy all the time," each one prayed a short prayer. A few tears were shed.

❧

MANY GUILT FEELINGS SURFACE WHILE RAISING A FAMILY. JOE'S BIRTHDAY PARTY PROVED TO US THAT EVEN OUR FEEBLEST EFFORTS ARE REWARDED.

56

I Checked under the Bed

I'm not sure what year the Charles Lindbergh baby was kidnapped, I think it was around the mid-1930s. But I do remember what this did to me as a child.

Our family received a local newspaper, so we were spared many of the gruesome details. However, when I visited my grandparents, I was exposed to Philadelphia's *Evening Bulletin.* Pictures of the Lindbergh home, the window, the ladder, the blond boy, and his parents were splashed across the paper like a photo album. That ladder, used for kidnapping the child from his bedroom crib, and stories of the ransom note helped make this an unforgettable plot. I gravitated toward anything associated with this story.

Publication of these vivid pictures and their stories "unbalanced" me. I remember peering out all my bedroom windows at night to see if a ladder might be propped against the house. Just to make sure no one had preceded me to my room, I checked under the bed. The fear this tragedy created in me lasted long after the story died. I had only seen still photos and heard the story on radio. How fortunate I never saw the horrible details on television! Eventually, peace did come. My nightly ritual ceased. God took away my fears.

ﻬ

IT IS LIBERATION TO LIE DOWN IN PEACE.

No Trial Run

PROVERBS 31:28

"Her children arise and call her blessed; her husband also, and he praises her."

According to the cards and poems for Mother's Day, mothers are hardly human. They give love endlessly. They understand. They are always there when needed.

Either children have short memories, or life is kind in allowing them to forget. My husband claims he was spanked by his mother almost daily, with various forms of application. My mother considered a 12-inch ruler a handy object for swift contact. I found the palm of my hand quite handy.

Do children forget that mothers seldom see past the hole in a new pair of trousers to a bruised knee? Even a numb, cold hand is neglected with the knowledge of a lost mitten. Many a tired mother will mete out punishment in proportion to her weary spirits. Mothers laugh, cry, despair, sing, and sulk. They raise children without a trial run. Each child is a new experience. Mothers do need empathy.

❧

PROVERBS 31:29

"Many women do noble things, but you surpass them all."

PROVERBS 31:29 IS A DIFFICULT PASSAGE TO ACCEPT WHEN YOU'RE WIPING RUNNY NOSES OR CHANGING SOGGY DIAPERS!

Children in the Temple Area

MATTHEW 21:15

"But when the chief priests and the teachers of the law saw the wonderful things he did and the children shouting in the temple area, 'Hosanna to the Son of David,' they were indignant."

MATTHEW 21:16

" 'Do you hear what these children are saying?' they asked him. 'Yes,' replied Jesus, 'have you never read, "From the lips of children and infants you have ordained praise"?' "

At four weeks old our babies made their first appearance at church. Except for illness, the children were present every Sunday thereafter. There was no nursery and no room that even resembled one.

The diaper bag was packed with the church service in mind—no loud rattles or noisy toys. A favorite was a string of beads made with puffed rice or puffed wheat. Sometimes eatables were put into tiny bottles. Shaking out the contents kept the baby busy while the preacher preached.

A clean handkerchief was a versatile object. A hankie could be folded to a triangle, then rolled from each end and magically turned into "babies in a swing." The twins could be rocked back and forth until they unrolled. Also a hankie could be laid flat and rolled tightly towards the center from both ends. With a little know-how of hankie art, this could be turned into a man.

Admittedly, sometimes our children were noisy or sang too loud, but we knew of no other way.

ॐ

JESUS WELCOMED CHILDREN IN THE "TEMPLE AREA."

59

A Toddler's Playpen

HEBREWS 12:7

"Endure hardship as discipline; God is treating you as sons. For what son is not disciplined by his father?"

It is only since my children are grown that I realize how far amiss I went with child psychology. I was not informed that almost any faulty character trait could be traced to how a child was toilet trained. I didn't start young, but when I did I meant business—having no concern for warping their personality.

I also kept them in a playpen, even after they could walk. I was unaware of stifling their exploratory urges which needed release. When I went out to hang up wash, I couldn't worry about the baby pulling the hot iron off the ironing board. Maybe my firm toilet training and limited freedom produced some quirks, but some of the modern methods aren't too convincing either.

Every person must learn to live within limitations. If he doesn't learn it young, his adult life is a catastrophe. A playpen, gate or fence may be a child's first introduction to life's limits.

HEBREWS 12:11

"No discipline seems pleasant at the time, but painful. Later on, however, it produces a harvest of righteousness and peace for those who have been trained by it."

❧

GOD'S DISCIPLINE MAY BE NO MORE WELCOME THAN A TODDLER'S PLAYPEN.

60

Basketballs, Footballs, and Baseball Gloves

GENESIS 2:24

"For this reason a man will leave his father and mother and be united to his wife, and they will become one flesh."

After preparing for the weddings of our three oldest daughters, I considered a son's wedding a breeze—no dresses to make, no meal to cater, no housecleaning to worry about. Besides providing refreshments for the rehearsal party, my only job was to present names and addresses for the wedding invitations. I had feared that Joe would marry a girl without a mother, and I'd be caught in the middle of another wedding.

It takes years after a child leaves home to find all the things that belong to him—basketballs, footballs, baseball gloves, a pair of outgrown ice skates in the old wood chest, his sleeping bag under the Ping-Pong table, a camouflaged army poncho for rain, and the electric train in a basement closet.

If these are the only things Joe took with him from our home, the 24 years spent there were a waste.

EPHESIANS 6:4

"Fathers, do not exasperate your children; instead, bring them up in the training and instruction of the Lord."

❧

TRAINING, LOVE, AND PRAYERS CANNOT BE PACKED INTO BOXES.

The Crab Apple Tree

To climb a crab apple tree seems like small joy. But for my daughter Libby and her friend Kim, the crab apple tree was the highlight of the summer. It was not our tree. It belonged to our neighbors, a retired pastor and his wife. The girls spent many hours in that tree, dreaming and "making believe"—even crawling into the tree with ice to make their own "air conditioning." Though it was not a large tree, they saw the world from a higher level.

The two girls, now grown women, have fond memories of these neighbors who gave their permission for this creative play. Instead of chasing the girls away, which they could have done, they allowed the crab apple tree to be their play sanctuary. It was definitely an important part of their growing up.

Many will remember the pastor for his visitation ministry and his sermons in local churches. For Libby and Kim, however, they will always cherish the memory of this pastor allowing them to play in the crab apple tree.

❧

THIS STORY OF LIBBY, KIM, AND THE CRAB APPLE TREE WAS READ AT THE PASTOR'S MEMORIAL SERVICE.

"Jimmys" Need Examples

DEUTERONOMY 6:6-7

"These commandments that I give to you today are to be upon your hearts. Impress them on your children. Talk about them when you sit at home and when you walk along the road, when you lie down and when you get up."

TITUS 2:6-8a

"Similarly, encourage the young men to be self-controlled. In everything set them an example by doing what is good. In your teaching show integrity, seriousness and soundness of speech that cannot be condemned."

A customer brought her small son into our store. He had taken an article from our store the previous week. She asked me if I would talk to him. The little fellow came into the office—alone. His head was hanging remorsefully. I felt sorry for him—also for his mother. An experience like this has a mother's heart pounding too.

"Jimmy" kept standing there looking at the blue carpet. After telling him what a little thing like this could lead to, I tried to impress upon him what a good mother I thought he had. His mother cared enough to bring him back and have him tell what happened. I prayed with him. I'm sure he left our store with a lighter load than when he came in. He even helped me pick up some books that I knocked down from a stock cart.

But there are adults who stuff their suitcases when they leave the hospital. Adults pilfer from their employers. Adults take home thick towels from motels. What can they say to their "Jimmys"?

❧

THERE ARE MANY "JIMMYS" WHO NEED GOOD EXAMPLES TO FOLLOW.

Take the Time

DEUTERONOMY 32:7a

"Remember the days of old; consider the generations long past."

I have many fond memories of having corn roasts at my childhood home. Only someone who made a living from rocks would have put eight tons of beautiful stone into an outdoor fireplace—which my father did. We had an oven in the chimney where we baked potatoes. Pounds and pounds of steak were made on that fireplace—and corn by the bushel. We didn't have a cozy dinner for six or eight; it wouldn't have been worth setting up the big folding table and long benches for so few. We had whole families of 20 or 30 enjoy our cook-out cuisine.

Last summer, at our son's request, we made roasted corn over our campfire, "like grandpop used to make." We tore off the dark green husks, pulled the tender husks down, and removed the silk. After arranging the light green husks around the cob again, we laid them on heavy duty foil placed over the grill. We wound up with roasting ears just as we remembered. As my father would have said, "It tastes just like roasted chestnuts." The grandchildren are now hearing of the good old days of our children.

❧

CHILDREN LOVE STORIES OF "HOW IT WAS WHEN WE WERE LITTLE." WE NEED TO TAKE THE TIME TO TELL THEM.

DEUTERONOMY 32:7b

"Ask your father and he will tell you, your elders, and they will explain to you."

God in Travel

PHILIPPIANS 2:4-5

"Each of you should look not only to your own interests, but also to the interests of others. Your attitude should be the same as that of Christ Jesus."

Weary Pilgrims

PHILIPPIANS 2:3

"Do nothing out of selfish ambition or vain conceit, but in humility consider others better than yourselves."

Christian booksellers from all over the country weighted down with Polaroids, Instamatics, and cassette recorders took off across the great Atlantic to Spain, Rome, and the Holy Land. Flight attendants catered to our every need. Being bussed to and from airports, delayed flights, and drastic security measures, plus the worry of passports tested the patience of many of us.

Finally, we arrived at our hotel in Madrid—exhausted. We were informed to check in, eat, and be ready to board our tour bus as quickly as possible. To look at a bed and realize you didn't dare go near it, to stare in the mirror and see yourself as everyone else would see you for the rest of the day sent a wave of depression over the most emotionally stable among us. Informed later to have our luggage in the hall by 4:30 the next morning, I dutifully complied—a sign of my disciplined upbringing.

I had chosen to go on this trip. However, I was not adjusting to this pilgrimage. I wanted to travel at my own pace, according to my own schedule.

PHILIPPIANS 2:4-5

"Each of you should look not only to your own interests, but also to the interests of others. Your attitude should be the same as that of Christ Jesus."

❧

WE ARE ONLY TOURISTS ON EARTH, BUT WHAT BETTER ADVICE FOR OUR JOURNEY.

Flying Is the Only Way to Go?

Right after New Year, bosses and their spouses think of taking off for somewhere—anywhere. I speak as the boss's wife, and I can tell you it would be easier to stay at home. Three weeks of paychecks must be taken care of, letters of cancellation sent to sales representatives, making sure deposits are made regularly and disbursements mailed to our suppliers. They make no allowances in their terms for a three-week vacation.

I'm never fond of flying. But when we're ready to leave and my husband starts telling the children where the insurance policies are and what to do should anything happen, I'm ready to forget the whole vacation. Like an expectant mother I want to ask, "Do I have to go through with this?"

"Flying is the only way to go," he comforts me, as he stuffs safety matches from the last motel in his pocket.

"Why did you do that?" I ask, as I fasten my seat belt.

"Well you never know when you need to send up flares," he remarks.

"We are flying over the ocean, remember?" I nervously jest. "Are you expecting to land on an oil slick?" In reality I am "fainthearted." With the jet streams behind us, I relax a bit as we level off.

❧

PSALM 53:5 IS EASY TO UNDERSTAND, AFTER A SAFE LANDING.

What Might Have Been

1 THESS. 5:16-18

"Be joyful always; pray continually; give thanks in all circumstances, for this is God's will for you in Christ Jesus."

We were parked in a rest area in Florida, planning on a quick lunch. In the compact kitchen of our trailer, I arranged tossed salad in shallow bowls. I was ready to open a can of shrimp to make it a salad supreme, when suddenly I was thrown to the floor. I was dashed back and forth till the trailer came to rest. Outside I heard my husband moan and call for someone to get me. I managed to get up amidst the debris and head for the door. There was a sea of pitch to greet me. I stepped into the mess with no thought of it being hot. Fortunately, I had sturdy shoes, and I was able to make it to the grass.

A tank truck containing hot roofing tar had hit us. It was lying on its side. I was bleeding from my forehead. I soon began to feel severe pain in my left rib area. Walter had been knocked back and forth between the car and the trailer. It was a miracle he was on his feet.

After many x-rays, five fractured ribs, and eight stitches, we achingly checked into a nearby motel. Dear friends, on hearing of our accident, stayed in the room across the hall. Two days later we flew home. When we realized "what might have been" we were grateful.

❧

MUCH CAN HAPPEN BETWEEN SUNRISE AND SUNSET WHICH DOES NOT IMMEDIATELY ENTERTAIN PRAISE.

PSALM 113:3

"From the rising of the sun to the place where it sets the name of the Lord is to be praised."

68

A Struggle with Humanity

PROVERBS 29:23

"A man's pride brings him low, but a man of lowly spirit gains honor."

After our accident do you know what I was thinking in the emergency room in Florida? I was so relieved that my hair was freshly washed. My favorite blue slacks were ruined by the hot pitch, but at least the nurses could see they sported a good label. I remembered I was wearing hose with runners, which didn't help my peace of mind. Why was I thinking such ridiculous thoughts when I didn't even know how seriously I was hurt?

How we laughed when our mothers and grandmothers made us change clothes so we'd look decent if we were in an accident! Surely, they knew an accident could be the ruination of our Sunday clothes. These were intelligent, serious women. They were also human. With this "handicap" they were overly concerned about how we appeared to others—even in an unforeseen event.

While writhing in pain these absurd thoughts filled my mind before I had time to classify them as vanity. My concern should have been more lofty during a crisis of this sort.

PSALM 103:13-14

"As a father has compassion on his children, so the Lord has compassion on those who fear him; for he knows how we are formed, he remembers that we are dust."

ठ

AS WE STRUGGLE WITH OUR HUMANITY, WHAT A CONSOLATION THAT GOD REMEMBERS!

Known Only to This Century

ISAIAH 40:22

"He sits enthroned above the circle of the earth, and its people are like grasshoppers. He stretches out the heavens like a canopy, and spreads them out like a tent to live in."

Through no manipulation of our own, we wound up in first class, headed for Los Angeles. For breakfast a white cloth napkin was spread on our tray, and orange juice was served in stemware. We were discussing the good fortune of this first-class luxury when my pessimistic husband declared, "Maybe they needed someone to balance the plane."

When you are flying at 39,000 feet, you have a different view of America. Instead of looking *across* the country, you are looking *down* on it. Over the prairie we see perfect circles of green, as if made with a compass, the result of irrigation. We continue over contour farming land, creating more beautiful patterns than an abstract artist can paint. Other areas resemble a crazy-patch quilt stretched out below us. The Arizona desert area has as many shades of brown as the East has shades of green.

Crossing the life-giving Colorado River, we soon fly over the Mojave Desert. Less than one hour later we see a city of green grass, swimming pools, and red roofs. In five hours of flying time, we have crossed our country to Los Angeles—a phenomenon known only to this century.

ISAIAH 66:1a

"This is what the Lord says: 'Heaven is my throne and the earth is my footstool.'"

❧

SOMEDAY WE MAY VACATION ON MARS. EVEN THIS BIT OF ACHIEVEMENT WOULD MAKE THE LORD CHUCKLE.

70

God in the Ordinary

1 TIMOTHY 6:6-7

"But godliness with contentment is great gain. For we brought nothing into the world and we can take nothing out of it."

No Rent, but Content

PROVERBS 15:16

"Better a little with the fear of the Lord than great wealth with turmoil."

The dilapidated house stood against a backdrop of well-grazed hills. Sheep, with black faces, nibbled the grass. A creek and a swinging bridge separated this home from an imposing world. The rainspout was propped up with an upside-down bathtub. Ducks and geese were in separate coops along the fence. In a pen was a 10-year-old raccoon the family has sheltered since its first few weeks of life.

A white-haired woman greeted us. She had lived there 50 years and raised 13 children. She paid no rent, except to look after the sheep and the property. I tried to imagine how many trips were made over the swinging bridge, how many bags of feed for her animals, how many bags of groceries.

"Do her children come home?" I asked.

"Oh yes, she has raised a fine family. A single daughter lives with her," our friend remarked. I saw transportation on the far side of the creek.

We chatted for a while with the octogenarian. As we cautiously stepped our way back over the weatherbeaten boards and rusty cables, I viewed the setting again in disbelief. I respected this woman, almost to the point of envy, for such contentment.

1 TIMOTHY 6:6-7

"But godliness with contentment is great gain. For we brought nothing into the world and we can take nothing out of it."

❧

CONTENTMENT IS NOT A SETTING, BUT A CONDITION OF THE HEART.

72

A Millionaire— but No Money

MATTHEW 6:19

"Do not store up for yourselves treasures on earth, where moth and rust destroy, and where thieves break in and steal."

PSALM 37:16

"Better the little that the righteous have than the wealth of many wicked."

We were hiking up the mountain. Leaves were thick and twigs and limbs lay across the path. Our friend looked at the ground and said, "Here are deer tracks." I marveled. How could he tell anything had traveled there? We climbed farther, whereupon he informed us the deer had changed its mind, turned, and gone the other way. By this time I was searching for tracks too.

I spotted some purple berries. "They are only good to eat after frost," our guide informed us. He was surprised we did not know the Pennsylvania Dutch name for them. He had the same friendship with trees; he could call them by name. He understood the seasons of bird migrations.

Remarking that he hunts only with a camera, he related how he spends his week of vacation during hunting season: he goes to the cabin he built on his farm and treats the hunters to hot dogs and sauerkraut.

As we were leaving, I said, "You are a wealthy man!"

"Yes," he replied, "That's what I tell people. I'm a millionaire. I just don't have the money."

ૐ

AT HIS ROADSIDE VEGETABLE STAND OUR FRIEND'S MONEY CUP WAS UNATTENDED.

73

Compulsive Doodling

JOHN 8:6b

"But Jesus bent down and started to write on the ground with his finger."

I'm a compulsive doodler. It's a pity I'm not famous because then I could sell my doodles. When I have a pencil in hand, I doodle on the phone book, calendar, or whatever will lend itself to doodling. Even the first draft of my writing usually looks like a giant doodle. I cross out words, write sideways, and insert new words here and there. It's a long way from the finished manuscript.

I wonder why doodlers doodle? Do we lack something? Do we have this impelling force to create? I have always doodled. I had a fancy doodle I used in school at the finish of an assignment. I felt it was not complete until my own special doodle signified the end. Doodling may not be the most profitable way of spending one's time. Some people walk to think, I doodle while I think. There's no medium to compare with good old pencil and paper.

Jesus was dealing with a tough question. Many people today show concern about what he wrote on the ground with his finger.

JOHN 8:7-8

"When they kept on questioning him, he straightened up and said to them, 'If any of you is without sin, let him be the first to throw a stone at her.' Again he stooped down and wrote on the ground."

❧

JESUS ANSWERED THE INTELLECTUALS VERBALLY. I THINK WHAT HE WROTE ON THE GROUND WAS DOODLING.

Leeks, Onions, and Garlic

More than 50 years have passed since our Swedish neighbors crossed the Atlantic and made America their home. During the Winter Olympics they were cheering the Swedish hockey team on to a bronze medal. They could rattle off every medal the Swedes had won—down to the exact meter or kilometer of the race.

Our friends read a Swedish newspaper, which occasionally finds its way into our mailbox by mistake. They enjoy limpa, a Swedish rye bread. They have me scrubbing my potatoes with an ingenious Swedish brush. For a hoarse throat, I soothe it with Lakerol—a licorice lozenge from Sweden. Our neighbors tell of Sweden's winters, far surpassing our cold weather.

Atmospheric conditions have little to do with the place we call home. Home is where you spend your childhood, even if it only represents one fifth of your life. It's not just a particular house—but a neighborhood, a town, a city, or a country. Home is where you made your first friends, played with your schoolmates. Home is where memories were born.

ಶ

IN RETROSPECT, THE LEEKS, ONIONS, AND GARLIC SEEM LIKE GOURMET FARE, AND SOMETIMES OUR MINDS EXAGGERATE THE GOOD TIMES.

75

High Price for Luxury

ECCLESIASTES 5:12a

"The sleep of a laborer is sweet, whether he eats little or much."

The need for aerobics, jogging, brisk walking, and all other forms of exercise is simple: we don't do what we once did. If you ever mowed an acre of lawn with a push lawn mower, you know the results were the same as a steam cabinet.

We could have used an aerobic record when we did the family wash. "Into the water and up to the wringer and into the water and up to the wringer." This same drill was repeated through two rinse waters. The bending exercise began when we stretched down to the basket and up to hang all those clothes on the line.

When have you seen a carpet on the line and a dedicated housewife toning up her muscles with a carpet beater? Or the living room furniture moved outdoors to clean? To cook a meal we no longer resemble a weight lifter—carrying a bucket of coal or an armload of wood.

After pushing the mower for a big lawn, no one needed to invest in jogging clothes. The labor required to do a big family wash left no spirit to compete in a tennis match.

INSOMNIA IS A HIGH PRICE TO PAY FOR LUXURY.

ECCLESIASTES 5:12b

"But the abundance of a rich man permits him no sleep."

God in the Past

JOB 38:36

"Who endowed the heart with wisdom or gave understanding to the mind?"

From Covered Wagon to a Space Shuttle

1 CORINTHIANS 1:20

"Where is the wise man? Where is the scholar? Where is the philosopher of this age? Has not God made foolish the wisdom of the world?"

What has happened in the past hundred years is difficult to comprehend. We have gone from the covered wagon to a space shuttle. The warmth of a wood stove in the kitchen has been replaced by the microwave. In the near future we will probably operate our microwaves by voice control. While traveling in our car, we will be able to pick up the phone and tell the microwave to shut off its refrigeration unit. Then we will instruct the microwave to defrost, to cook at a certain temperature, and to keep the food warm.

In this century we have advanced from the Morse Code to direct dialing, reaching many parts of the world. We have progressed from having no radios to battery-operated miniatures. Marconi himself would be astonished.

Computers will change our lives more than all the other inventions combined. Computers now control many of these previous inventions. Instead of the ordinary typewriter, a word processor can "remember" a whole manuscript. Bad spelling is no longer a problem. The dictionary within corrects mispelled words. Imagine!

JOB 38:36

"Who endowed the heart with wisdom or gave understanding to the mind?"

❧

"WHO ENDOWED THE HEART WITH WISDOM . . . ?" GOD DID.

78

The Well
I Remember

2 SAMUEL 23:15

"David longed for water and said, 'Oh, that someone would get me a drink of water from the well near the gate of Bethlehem!' "

PSALM 42:1-2

"As the deer pants for streams of water, so my soul pants for you, O God. My soul thirsts for God, for the living God. When can I go and meet with God?"

We had an old-fashioned well a few steps from our front porch. It was a favorite stop-off for swimmers on their way to the old swimming hole. A rusty tin cup, hanging on the porch post, added to the flavor of this refreshing water. A special treat was having a sawed-off coconut shell to use for a cup. The hairy exterior didn't detract from the water's "crispness."

The pavement surrounding the pump was a wonderful place to splash in water. Our pump pumped easy, so most any child could use it. On hot, humid days, bare feet thrilled as they sloshed under the rush of chilled water. It was difficult to keep children away from all this exciting potential.

Scrubbing our big porch was no problem. We didn't use a hose. It was only a few feet to the pump, so buckets of water were readily available. A well, so easily accessible, was a luxury. For an inanimate object, the pump seemed to possess a distinctive "personality," making our home more homey. It welcomed any thirsty passerby. Like David, I would enjoy a cool drink of water from the well I remember.

ès

AS FRESH WATER SOOTHES THE PARCHED LIPS OF A THIRSTY MAN, SO THE LIVING GOD SATISFIES A THIRSTY SOUL.

The Kitchen Couch

The couches of King Xerxes seem cold and forbidding. The kitchen couch in my memory was warm and inviting. The one end was raised to fit your resting head. The other end was flat with nothing to interfere with tired feet. A sick child could be laid on the kitchen couch so they could watch and be watched.

Old kitchens were friendly places. They were not designed strictly for the culinary arts. In addition to a couch my grandmother's kitchen was furnished with a rocking chair, a treadle sewing machine, an extension table, chairs, and a wood-and-coal-burning kitchen range. The oven door was opened and the babies were bathed on the mother's lap in the warm air that escaped. "Bonding" was being practiced long before there was a word for it.

A recliner could be our modern-day version of the couch. However, I haven't recently seen a kitchen designed to accommodate one. At one time the sophisticated living of our dens, rec rooms, and family rooms was all performed in the realm of the kitchen.

THE POPULAR CRY FOR "OUR OWN SPACE" HAS CREATED A SELF-IMPOSED ISOLATION WE WEREN'T EXPECTING.

80

Down Home, Up Home, Over Home

PSALM 16:5

"Lord, you have assigned me my portion and my cup; you have made my lot secure."

"Down home" was where we lived with my father's parents until I was 12. "Up home" was three miles north, where we moved when my parents bought a home of their own. "Over home" lay to the northeast and was my mother's childhood home. It was at "over home" where I was educated in the knowledge of the past.

"Over home" had winding stairs—all three flights. The ground cellar was packed down to a smooth, hard floor. The only indoor plumbing was a pump at a tin-covered sink. A hand-powered washer, with the help of homemade soap, produced clean clothes only once a week. A "light plant" was a luxury that produced enough electricity to keep the light bulbs lit—though dim and flickering. Irons were heated on the kitchen range in the winter and the kerosene stove in the summer. An ironing board, padded with worn-out blankets and covered with muslin, was balanced on the back of a chair and a windowsill. Here shirts were ironed to perfection. My grandmother could make shoofly pies four inches high in her nonmechanical oven without a thermometer!

How fortunate to feel so close to three locations enough to call them all "home."

❧

OUR CHRISTIAN HERITAGE CANNOT BE SEPARATED FROM THE SURROUNDINGS IN WHICH IT WAS BORN.

PSALM 16:6

"The boundary lines have fallen for me in pleasant places; surely I have a delightful inheritance."

81

Ye Old-Time Gang

ECCLESIASTES 4:10

"If one falls down, his friends can help him up. But pity the man who falls and has no one to help him up!"

"Ye Old-Time Gang Reunion" is not a family reunion, but a group of couples we traveled with when we were single. Once a year we gather for a picnic. We eat, have fellowship, chat, reminisce, and keep posted on the children and grandchildren.

When we were younger we spent most of our dates with a couple from this group. We sang around the piano, had picnics, visited local "scenic wonders," drove to our favorite hamburger place, and on Sunday nights went somewhere to church.

Now when we gather, we still sing hymns around the piano, for old time's sake. Some who were tenors now sing bass. Many of us share the same problem of not being able to see the words. But we sing with the same gusto of 40 years ago.

"Ye Old-Time Gang" has remained closely knit. In times of sickness we share. Some of our group have moved out of state, but they are still remembered. One time a van was rented and the reunion was moved to a member's home in another state. Many times letters are read from absent members.

ਦੇ

IN COUNTING LIFE'S BLESSINGS, THIS CIRCLE OF FRIENDS WOULD BE NEAR THE TOP OF THE LIST.

ECCLESIASTES 4:12

"Though one may be overpowered, two can defend themselves. A cord of three strands is not quickly broken."

82

Milk Pie and Sour Gravy

ACTS 14:17b

"He has shown kindness by giving you rain from heaven and crops in their season; he provides you with plenty of food and fills your hearts with joy."

1 TIMOTHY 6:8

"But if we have food and clothing, we will be content with that."

My mother knew how to stretch food. I'm sure she learned it from her mother. We always seemed to have plenty. If she didn't have enough leftover potatoes to fry, bread was torn into a dish, moistened by an egg, then added to the frying potatoes. A vegetable could be increased by adding more milk which was thickened to a delicious creamed dish. Hamburgers were seldom made with all meat. A pound of ground meat could be increased to a few more patties by adding milk, eggs, and bread crumbs. Even from a "naked" bone, the most delicious vegetable soup emerged.

And milk pie, what a delicacy! Leftover pieces of dough were rerolled to fit a pie pan. It was filled with a mixture of flour, sugar, and milk—then dotted with butter and sprinkled with cinnamon. I doubt whether Julia Child's French pastries taste any better. Milk pie had many names. One of the most common was "slop pie." It did not deserve that name!

Recently, someone reminded me of sour gravy. My mother made it with bacon. My informant said they just browned flour in lard, added water, sugar, and vinegar. And we remember these dishes "with joy."

≥⋟

Do We Enjoy Too Much of Everything Today?

Old Wives' Tales

1 TIMOTHY 4:7

"Have nothing to do with godless myths and old wives' tales; rather, train yourself to be godly."

We were not superstitious in our home. However, we had a grandmother living with us who believed in superstitions. She would not allow us to sweep the dirt out the door. In doing so, she contended, you would sweep your luck right with it. Opening an umbrella in the house was equally destructive to your good luck.

Babies were also the object of superstitions. A tiny baby taking a ride in the car could become "liver-grown" (whatever that meant). Under Grammy's supervision, we handed our poor Rosie around the table leg three times to loosen up her liver. To this day, I wince when someone steps over a baby on the floor, because Grammy said they would stop growing.

She followed the almanac religiously. I remember if you planted in the "sign of Blume frau" your plants would have only flowers, but no vegetables.

If you threw the hair from your comb outside, and if the birds used it for a nest, you would get a headache.

Many superstitions are connected with bad luck: a black cat, a broken mirror, walking under a ladder, the number 13.

❧

PSALM 37:3

"Trust in the Lord and do good; dwell in the land and enjoy safe pasture."

WITH THIS VERSE IN MIND, WHY DO CHRISTIANS GIVE "OLD WIVES' TALES" A SECOND THOUGHT?

84

The Hometown Paper

PROVERBS 27:8

"Like a bird that strays from its nest is a man who strays from his home."

When do you stop the hometown paper? We've lived in Allentown almost 40 years and still subscribe to my husband's hometown paper—the *Souderton Independent*. It's not a take-it-or-leave-it situation, either. Walt is disappointed when delivery is delayed for a day or two. He enjoys it from page one.

I check on the weddings and anniversaries—also the obituaries. My concern with the deaths is directly related to an intense interest in their ages. I rarely know the new brides and grooms, but their parents' or grandparents' names may be familiar.

I remember when rural area reporters were housewives. In their own "journalese" they reported who were the Sunday dinner guests of our neighbors and revealed our whereabouts in the same column. (When did we stop caring about who visited who on Sunday?) The local newspapers published when friends were admitted to the hospital—and when discharged. The weekly announcements of the "population growth" created great interest.

To maintain sanity, in this time of sophisticated news and intellectual journalism, I think our contact through the hometown paper is necessary.

ISAIAH 46:9

"Remember the former things, those of long ago; I am God, and there is no other; I am God, and there is none like me."

❧

WE CANNOT OVERESTIMATE THE INFLUENCE OF THE FOLKS IN OUR HOMETOWN.

Sunday Was a Day of Rest

EXODUS 34:21

"Six days you shall labor, but on the seventh day you shall rest; even during the plowing season and harvest you must rest."

V*acation* was not a commonplace word in my childhood vocabulary. Work started early in the morning and continued until dusk. Many summer days were concluded after 15 hours of work.

Making hay without the modern equipment was no picnic. The hay was mowed with a mowing machine. It was raked with a hayrake and forked on the wagon with long-handled forks. Then it was hoisted into the mow with a hayhook, operated by a pulley, powered by a rope attached to the tractor. Later in the summer the harvest of wheat and oats required even more work.

However, sitting on the wicker rockers after the sun had set was more relaxing than driving 150 miles to lounge on a chair. Smelling honeysuckles at the edge of the porch, catching fireflies, and dodging bats was enough diversion to unwind the whole family before bedtime. And no matter how busy we were, Sunday was a day of rest. Only the essential chores were performed.

From the Beginning the Lord Planned the Equivalent of More Than a Seven-Week Vacation—52 Days a Year.

GENESIS 2:3

"And God blessed the seventh day and made it holy, because on it he rested from all the work of creating that he had done."

Ask the Former Generations

JOB 8:8-9

"Ask the former generations and find out what their fathers learned, for we were born only yesterday and know nothing, and our days on earth are but a shadow."

Today's ecologists could save a lot of time if they sat down and talked with their grandmothers. Grandmas had recycling down to a science. Bread wrappers were used instead of a roll of wax paper. Every home had a ball of string saved from their groceries. It would have been unthinkable to throw brown bags aways and then buy lunch bags. Mustard jars, mayonnaise jars, and most any other jars were stored and used for jelly. Shredded Wheat cards were saved on which children could express their artistic flair. When the first day of the month arrived, the old month was torn off the calendar and the back used for scrap paper. Old newspapers were used to line drawers, cupboards, and chests. "Don't waste," was a familiar phrase.

ₑ

"FORMER GENERATIONS" HAD THE ANSWER TO MORE THAN ECOLOGY.

JOB 8:10

"Will they not instruct you and tell you? Will they not bring forth words from their understanding?"

God in Christmas and Easter

LUKE 2:18

"And all who heard it were amazed at what the shepherds said to them."

Serendipity!

LUKE 2:10

"But the angel said to them, 'Do not be afraid. I bring you good news of great joy that will be for all the people.' "

Somewhere in the Christmas rush there must be serendipity—"the gift of finding valuable things not sought for." At this frantic time I don't know what I seek, but I sure could use some happy surprises—like finding out I slept through the first 24 days of December. Think of all the frayed nerves I'd avoid. In the tale of Rip Van Winkle, his 20-year snooze made him miss the Revolutionary War and the passing of his nagging wife.

Since serendipity is a gift of finding valuable things not sought for, I can't go looking for it. It's finding the unheard-of where you least expect it. If an unreasonable customer surprises me by acting civil—serendipity! If you open an envelope and find a check where you expected a bill—that's serendipity! Or you gaze on a sheet of beautiful, browned cookies instead of burned ones—yes, serendipity!

Shepherds too busy to go to Bethlehem would have missed the surprise in the stable, not to mention the chance of the centuries.

WE CAN'T DO ANYTHING TO FIND SERENDIPITY. LET'S NOT BE TOO BUSY TO RECOGNIZE IT WHEN IT COMES.

LUKE 2:18

"And all who heard it were amazed at what the shepherds said to them."

A Lavish Gift

PROVERBS 15:29

"The Lord is far from the wicked but he hears the prayer of the righteous."

A woman was resting on a chair next to the desk where my son was working in our bookstore. Joe got up to attend to some business. When he returned she asked, "May I speak to you? I'm 95 years old. I used to love to read and do things for the Lord but now my services are limited. I heard recently of all the shoplifting that goes on. While you were gone, I felt a burden to pray for the protection and ministry of this store, because all these religious items are so useful."

He was touched by her concern. "Her disposition was so beautiful," he commented. "I felt like an angel had visited us."

This woman had captured the spirit of the Christmas season. She was sharing her remaining gift—prayer. A gift that was seemingly insignificant was indeed lavish!

DEUTERONOMY 16:17

"Each of you must bring a gift in proportion to the way the Lord your God has blessed you."

❧

MANY OF US WILL NEVER MATCH OUR ELDERLY FRIEND'S GENEROSITY.

With Joyful Songs

PSALM 148:12-13

". . . young men and maidens, old men and children. Let them praise the name of the Lord, for his name alone is exalted; his splendor is above the earth and the heavens."

When our youngest was a member of her school choir, we listened to "Messiah" by Handel. She brought a cassette home to learn her alto part. I heard nothing but an alto solo for a solid evening. Libby, who usually had a different taste in music than mine, became completely absorbed with classical Christmas music. What I could not accomplish, the choir director of our public high school did.

After attending four concerts, I also knew those songs. I sat there and hyperventilated along with the kids. If one had fainted on stage, I would probably have collapsed in my seat. Once when our son sang in his Christmas concert, he began yawning and turned pale in the middle of a majestic piece. It was a close call.

None of our five children entered a musical career. There was not a musical genius among them. However, the experience of choir practice, being introduced to great religious music, and singing their best at a concert, was time well spent. How could anyone who sang the "Hallelujah Chorus" ever forget it?

THAT INCLUDES MONOTONES, TOO.

PSALM 100:2

"Serve the Lord with gladness; come before him with joyful songs."

Christ in Christmas

LUKE 2:11

"Today in the town of David a Savior has been born to you; he is Christ the Lord."

I t's a tough job trying to make Christmas nonreligious. My sympathy for the choir director who must plan a Christmas program without carols. And school bands—imagine Christmas without hearing the brass sound the notes of "Joy to the World."

Who wants Christmas without stars? No Mary, no Joseph, no stable, no Wise Men? A secularized Christmas would never use, "Peace on earth good will toward men."

To eliminate Christ from Christmas you would have to destroy all the evidence— including the Michelangelos, the Rembrandts, Reubens, and da Vincis, the works of Beethoven, Haydn, Bach, Mozart, and Handel. To search for the millions of Bibles, translated into many languages and distributed around the world, would take quite a force. The job would be too big for the FBI, the KGB, and Scotland Yard combined. Those who oppose a religious Christmas will enjoy only limited success.

LUKE 2:14

"Glory to God in the highest, and on earth peace, good will toward men" (KJV).

❧

THERE'S NO WAY OF UNDOING 2000 YEARS.

93

An Earthly Grand Finale

Crosses are everywhere. They are worn on chains around the neck, carried in pockets, hoisted to the top of church steeples, and illuminated so they shine in the dark. On my desk is a pencil holder with three crosses carved by laser beam. The cross has been the religious symbol of the centuries.

Today, crosses are made of sanded wood and polished brass. The original was no doubt full of splinters and splattered with blood. A cross necklace would not sell well if it was an authentic copy. We have brassed it, silvered it, gilded it, and studded it with diamonds—shrouding its meaning. An imprisoned pastor declared of the cross, "It was a battleground. It was the place of the bitterest conflict in world history." There is no way to glamorize the cross. It is a symbol of suffering, blood, and death—hardly captured in 14K gold.

ξ❧

YES, EASTER BRINGS HOPE! THE RESURRECTION IS AN EARTHLY GRAND FINALE TO CHRIST'S BIRTH, LIFE, AND DEATH.

God in Our Conduct

PSALM 33:13-15

"From heaven the Lord looks down and sees all mankind; from his dwelling place he watches all who live on the earth—he who forms the hearts of all, who considers everything they do."

Where Is God?

"But if I go to the east, he is not there; if I go to the west, I do not find him. When he is at work in the north, I do not see him; when he turns to the south, I catch no glimpse of him."

"From heaven the Lord looks down and sees all mankind; from his dwelling place he watches all who live on the earth—he who forms the hearts of all who considers everything they do."

We are news-saturated! We get the local morning paper, a New York daily, and a weekly national news magazine. Sometimes we watch two television newscasts. One push button is set to an all-news station on the car radio. Any one of these media is enough to keep us posted on what we need to know about current events.

Why do we torment ourselves with all the depressing news? It's like an obsession. We listen to the 10:00 or 11:00 news to hear repeated what we heard at 6:00 or 6:30. The next morning we hurry to read the morning paper, still in our nightclothes.

Stunned by all this shocking news, people cry, "Where is God in all of this? Why doesn't he do something? If God cared for us, he would not let this happen."

≥

FROM HIS VANTAGE POINT GOD MUST BE ASKING A FEW QUESTIONS TOO.

Tending Cattle on the High Seas

MATTHEW 25:35

"For I was hungry and you gave me something to eat, I was thirsty and you gave me something to drink, I was a stranger and you invited me in."

MATTHEW 25:40

"The King will reply, 'I tell you the truth, whatsoever you did for one of the least of these brothers of mine, you did it for me.'"

In 1946, at age 44, my father boarded a cattle boat bound for Poland. The ship was loaded with cattle to help this war-ridden country. My father was prone to seasickness. I remember praying intensely that he maintain his equilibrium. Our prayers were answered—not one day of vertigo during his weeks at sea.

Recent years have made us aware of the terrible Holocaust which preceded my father's trip. I found solace in the fact that at least one person close to me had tried to relieve the ravages of war.

My father was too young to be drafted in World War I, and too old in World War II. He was a man of deep faith and sensitivity. He was opposed to war. However, he felt an obligation to do something constructive. In a small way, his tending of cattle on the high seas helped to fulfill this indebtedness.

❧

THE MASS DESTRUCTION OF WAR COULD NOT BE OVERCOME BY A CARGO OF CATTLE ABOARD A SHIP, BUT IF EACH OF US PUT INTO ACTION THE SAME KIND OF CONSCIENTIOUS EFFORT, THE POSSIBILITY OF FUTURE HOLOCAUSTS WOULD DIMINISH.

What a Life!

EPHESIANS 6:2

" 'Honor your father and mother'— which is the first commandment with a promise . . ."

When the washing machine broke, he didn't know how to fix it. His cars seemed to run forever—without the usual tune-ups. My father was a "people person," even with the pressures of business. He always had time to talk. It would tax my brain to try and remember a single enemy. He could communicate with equal freedom to the Governor of Arizona or to Jimmy Webb who lived in a shack near our home. My father did not know how to put on airs.

He was sparse with his reprimands. I remember only one spanking. Our old sow named Peg felt his gentleness as he helped her through the birth of her many litters of piglets. He appeared fearless when he checked the strange noises we heard at night. His natural bent toward doctoring was well-utilized during our childhood sniffles, coughs, and fevers. He transposed the message of the Bible into everyday life.

When he died from cancer at the age of 61, I thought, "What a death!" Whereupon I had to add, "What a life!"

&

MY FATHER OFTEN REPEATED PROVERBS 4:23 FROM MEMORY.

PROVERBS 4:23

"Keep thy heart with all diligence, for out of it are the issues of life" (KJV).

98

A Rained-Out Picnic

ROMANS 8:28

"And we know that in all things God works for the good of those who love him, who have been called according to his purpose."

With 13 rainy weekends out of 14, we should have expected rain. The Pocono Mountains were like a rain forest. Our preparations for a family picnic on Memorial Day weekend went soggy. I lay in bed trying to plan our strategy, while the rain beat down on the trailer roof. How could I make all that chicken in our trailer? My oven was surely too small. Fifteen of us were expected to gather under our dripping canopy.

I finally decided to cook the chicken in a big pot before church and then fry it at noon. If by accident the sun did smile on us we could follow through with our original plans. Our son-in-law would not hear of frying the chicken in a pan, so he and my husband donned their rain suits and finished it to perfection over the wood fire.

Monday's weather was like leftovers from Sunday—until the afternoon. While we were driving home from our holiday weekend, we had to wear sunglasses.

ֶ

A RAINED-OUT PICNIC SEEMS TRITE. BUT ON THE DAY IT HAPPENS, IT COMES CLOSE TO BEING "AFFLICTION."

LAMENTATIONS 3:33

"For he does not willingly bring affliction or grief to the children of men."

Mine Is a Solo Act

1 CORINTHIANS 4:9a

"For it seems to me that God has put us apostles on display at the end of the procession, like men condemned to die in the arena."

Shakespeare was right when he said, "All the world's a stage." You can see more drama in one day of real life than in a week of stage production.

Several years ago a man climbed the Reunion Tower in Dallas, Texas. From a ledge he threw notes to the ground telling people to love each other. We were in Dallas at the time but missed the whole production.

My favorite "theater" is the hotel lobby—where all men and women are players. If you can't hear them speak, it's like watching mime. Playwrights must get their inspiration for small talk in hotel lobbies. The best comedies in the world are performed here in gowns, tuxedos, sneakers, swimsuits, western hats, and overalls. My amusement is held in perspective when I remember that on this stage, I am a player, too. In the eyes of the rest of the "cast," mine is a solo act.

ॐ

SOMETIMES MY INTEREST IN THE PERFORMANCE OF OTHERS CAUSES ME TO NEGLECT MY OWN.

1 CORINTHIANS 4:9b

"We have been made a spectacle to the whole universe, to angels as well as to men."

Do It with All Your Might

2 THESSALONIANS 3:10

"For even when we were with you we gave you this rule: 'If a man will not work, he shall not eat.' "

At our Pocono campground my husband is known for his extraordinary campfires. More than one polyester shirt has holes to substantiate the above statement! A diminishing woodpile on our campsite causes him such a bout of insecurity remedied only by several wheelbarrow-loads of wood. When neighbors create a hissing, snapping fire, they dub it a "Walt's Fire."

Several years ago, I bought him a new ax. I was so frightened by the flying wood, I was glad to see the ax quickly retired. Later we found a simple splitter, with a steel handle. Less effort is required to ready the wood for the fire, and it is far safer.

A weekend at our campfire can leave you smelling like a smokehouse. When I dump the clothes on our basement floor, the full impact hits me. I realize how we must have smelled as we were shopping or attending church.

The way a man builds a fire tells something about him. My husband builds fires the way he works—intensely.

ঽ

SOME OF LIFE'S ISSUES MAY NOT HAVE CLEAR-CUT ANSWERS IN THE BIBLE, BUT WORK IS NOT ONE OF THEM.

ECCLESIASTES 9:10a

"Whatever your hand finds to do, do it with all your might."

One-Half Cup of Sourdough

LUKE 6:38

*"Give, and it will
be given to you. A
good measure,
pressed down,
shaken together and
running over, will
be poured into your
lap. For with the
measure you use, it
will be measured to
you."*

After tasting the delicious sticky buns made with sourdough, one can understand why it was essential to the early settlers. It could be used for bread, pancakes, biscuits, and other goodies.

I was given less than a half cup of sourdough. According to the instructions, if I feed it right, I can keep it alive indefinitely. Sourdough is known to have stayed in a family for over 100 years. I must feed it every seven days or more often if I use it. Why I accepted the challenge to keep this dough alive is interesting—since another cactus of mine needs artificial respiration.

The person who gave me the sourdough seemed to think it gave one a feeling of security to have it available any time. I wondered if keeping track of its feeding schedule might be more concern than security. If I don't use the gift, it will keep fermenting and pop the lid— spreading sourdough all over my refrigerator. To preserve this gift, I must use it and share it.

❧

A FRESH LOAF OF SOURDOUGH BREAD IS FAR MORE CONVINCING THAN THE RECIPE.

JAMES 2:17

*"In the same way,
faith by itself, if it is
not accompanied by
action, is dead."*

Applause Means Approval?

PSALM 62:4b

"With their mouths they bless, but in their hearts they curse."

I'm beginning to think that complete silence is more of a compliment than applause. I've attended banquets which produced clapping 50 times. The master of ceremonies tells a joke—applause. The board of directors is introduced with their spouses—applause. More applause for those who worked behind the scenes. Let's not forget the waiters and waitresses who served the meal—even if the service was lousy. When the music for the evening is introduced—applause, and again when they sit down.

By the time the speaker steps to the podium, the audience may be ready to sleep or, like a stream of ants, weave in and out of the tables to the rest rooms. Others check or wind their watches while a few more crane their necks looking for a clock.

Applause means approval—right? Many times I've clapped when I didn't approve.

è&

PROVERBS 12:22

"The Lord detests lying lips, but he delights in men who are truthful."

LIES ARE NOT COMMUNICATED THROUGH THE LIPS ALONE.

Find Out What Pleases the Lord

EPHESIANS 5:11

"Have nothing to do with the fruitless deeds of darkness, but rather expose them."

I sat and watched a television show for an hour, expecting the story would have a message. It ended so abruptly, I could not decide what the whole thing was about. Aside from being frustrating, most of what appears on television is vulgar, immoral, and violent. Television has made us shallow thinkers. It is warping the minds of our children. As a destroyer of creativity, its destruction cannot be measured. I keep thinking, "What would my grandmother think of this 'monster' that has invaded our home?"

It is easy to become addicts. When we come home tired, the easiest thing is to grab the remote control and flip the switch.

Would I have watched the shows I am now watching 10 years ago? Or as Charles Sheldon asks in his book *In His Steps*—"What would Jesus do?"

EPHESIANS 5:8-10

"For you were once darkness, but now you are light in the Lord. Live as children of light (for the fruit of the light consists in all goodness, righteousness and truth) and find out what pleases the Lord."

ॐ

TO "FIND OUT WHAT PLEASES THE LORD" IN TODAY'S TELEVISION REQUIRES LITTLE DELIBERATION.

Behind the Wheel of a Car

PSALM 37:8

"Refrain from anger and turn from wrath; do not fret— it leads only to evil."

My husband says I'm a good driver. He even sleeps when I drive. However, I'm beginning to question my ability. According to the drivers I see in my rearview mirror, I have no right to the center lane when I want to make a left-hand turn. If I forget that I can now make a right-hand turn on red, I get a dirty look and an ear-splitting blast of the horn. These drivers must be wearing masks because real faces wouldn't appear so distorted.

Road construction produces irresponsibility. Drivers ignore sign after sign instructing them to "Form Single Lane," resulting in chaotic conditions.

All of us have accidently gone through a stop sign or turned onto a one-way street. We may not have seen a car coming because a shrub blocked our view, so we should have a little understanding for a stranger who is in the wrong lane. Traveling is too dangerous to be distracted by angry motorists.

❧

BEHIND THE WHEEL OF A CAR, REMAINING CALM IS QUITE AN ORDER!

COLOSSIANS 3:8

"But now you must rid yourselves of all such things as these: anger, rage, malice, slander, and filthy language from your lips."

Clear Conscience and Clean Hands

GENESIS 20:5

"Did he not say to me, 'She is my sister,' and didn't she say, 'He is my brother?' I have done this with a clear conscience and clean hands."

I know for sure you can be dead wrong when you think you are right! I stopped at a red light, pulled away on green, but the police car was flashing behind me. I drove to the side of the road unaware of my transgression. After the formality of the driver's license and owner's card routine, I asked the police officer, "What did I do?"

"You have the wrong inspection sticker," he replied flatly.

I looked in amazement to find my inspection was three days overdue. My number 2 should have been a number 4. Why hadn't my husband taken care of it as he usually did? I shouldn't have to concern myself with inspection stickers, oil pressure, or battery fluid! Like Abimelech, I had "clean hands"—I was placing the blame on someone else. Nevertheless, my breaking the law had to be rectified. I took the car directly to the inspection station. I was grateful there were no charges filed against me.

ಜಾ

TRUSTING A "CLEAR CONSCIENCE" IS NOT ALWAYS SAFE.

PSALM 32:2

"Blessed is the man whose sin the Lord does not count against him and in his spirit is no deceit."

106

Sin Is an Epidemic

LEVITICUS 13:46

"As long as he has the infection he remains unclean. He must live alone; he must live outside the camp."

Being quarantined was no fun. Measles, chicken pox, mumps, diptheria—any kind of communicable disease was quarantined. In the doorway of our home, the county health officer tacked the poster labeling our disease. It was a warning for those who approached.

My most memorable quarantine was for scarlet fever. My mother and I shared the rash. A month of isolation was an eternity for me, a second-grader. No one could come to see us, and we couldn't go anywhere. My two aunts were in the house when we were diagnosed, which automatically put them under quarantine for 10 days—in their own homes.

My grandfather, distraught by the fact that he might not be able to vote, moved his bed to their kitchen. Since we shared the same stairway and bathroom, it was difficult to isolate our germs. I remember my teacher visited me during this confinement and talked through the glass pane in the porch window. Before we could socialize again, this disease required fumigation.

A scarlet fever rash can hardly be compared to the spots of leprosy. However, for a symbol of sin, they both qualify.

1 JOHN 1:9

"If we confess our sins, he is faithful and just and will forgive us our sins and purify us from all unrighteousness."

❧

SIN IS AN EPIDEMIC. HOW FOOLISH NOT TO APPLY THE CURE.

Waiting Your Turn

PROVERBS 14:29

"A patient man has great understanding, but a quick-tempered man displays folly."

EPHESIANS 4:2

"Be completely humble and gentle; be patient, bearing with one another in love."

A doctor's office was like the barber shop—you waited your turn. If there was standing room only, you had to decide if your ill-health warranted the waiting. Our daughter Jenny remembers being sent in to save a seat while I parked the car. After taking a good look around, you tried to decide how many were ahead of you and how many belonged together. Controlling three little ones, while you waited your turn, was no small task—especially in the winter. It meant removing snowsuits, caps, mittens, boots, and later putting them back on.

However, our doctor did make house calls, and those high fevers were sometimes treated at home from the intriguing doctor's bag—filled with pills of every color and hue. A child is deprived who has not enjoyed an occasional house call!

Now we run by appointments only. Everything is scheduled. A 15-minute wait can cause a tremor in the waiting room. There are no allowances for delays in our schedules.

❧

CHRISTIAN CONDUCT HAS HIGH STANDARDS.

Seeds and Weeds

LUKE 8:7

"Other seed fell among thorns, which grew up with it and choked the plants."

I planted tomatoes, cauliflower, and brussels sprouts, but I raised weeds. You should have seen the variety! They were so hearty, they choked out everything but a few tomato plants. That garden gave me nothing but a guilt complex all summer. Every time I stepped out the back door, on both sides of the step, it looked like underbrush. I had weeds with blue flowers that would add character to any hanging basket. Other weeds looked like timothy hay. My "ground cover" was creeping crabgrass and chickweed. Only close observation revealed my stunted vegetables.

On Labor Day I put on my gloves and pulled out everything—tomatoes and all. The growth was so dense that all kinds of bugs and snails—or whatever they were—lived there. Even with gloves I wouldn't pick them up.

I probably reacted irrationally—there were some green tomatoes yet to ripen. However, to untangle the good from the bad was too much trouble. Besides, the "good" in this case was not the vegetables.

❧

"WORRIES, RICHES, AND PLEASURES" STILL CHOKE.

LUKE 8:14

"The seed that fell among thorns stands for those who hear, but as they go on their way they are choked by life's worries, riches and pleasures, and they do not mature."

Better One Handful

LUKE 12:15b

"Watch out! Be on your guard against all kinds of greed; a man's life does not consist in the abundance of his possessions."

We were married during World War II. New furniture and electrical appliances were at a premium—almost nonexistent. Our first living room suite was a rebuilt model. Our spare-room furniture was secondhand. Odd pieces were painted to match. The crib we used for all five children first cradled my sister. Later we purchased twin beds at the Rescue Mission. Accumulating this hodgepodge of furniture is probably the reason for what creativity our children may have had. Bureaus and beds had layers of paint, with anything from pink to lavender. I made floral sheets from feed bags long before designers made them popular.

It was many years before we disposed of the last Rescue Mission bed. It was our son Joe's bed till he married. Though not a piece in his bedroom belonged together, each piece told a story. The chest-of-drawers was the remaining piece from my parents original bedroom suite. The desk was a gift I gave Walter before we were married. On the rocker, given by my parents, I spent many sleepless hours in discomfort before Joe was born. All but the rocker is gone, and it now rests in the attic.

ECCLESIASTES 4:6 NEEDS NO EXPLANATION.

ECCLESIASTES 4:6

"Better one handful with tranquility than two handfuls with toil and chasing the wind."

110

God in Our Daily Walk

ROMANS 9:21

"Does not the potter have the right to make out of the same lump of clay some pottery for noble purposes and some for common use?"

A God Original

ROMANS 9:20

"Shall what is formed say to him who formed it, 'Why did you make me like this?' "

After quite a recess I started sewing for myself again. The first two dresses turned out fine. With the third one I threw the pattern away before the dress was hemmed. I started with beautiful material. I lined it. There was topstitching galore. I was proud of my sewing. Few designer dresses would have taken more hours.

I knew before it was finished it was not my style. However, I forced myself to finish it. The billowy sleeves and flouncy gathers looked great on the pattern, but hanging on me they looked a fright. I hoped the belt might pull in the lines. It didn't.

Not willing to donate my creation to a "worthy cause," I cut off the crocheted belt loops and opened the side seams at the waist. Threading the belt into the holes, I left the back hang and tied the belt in the front. It was a housecoat, a lined, well-made, expensive housecoat—a Ruth Hackman Original. Even more useful than a dress.

ROMANS 9:21

"Does not the potter have the right to make out of the same lump of clay some pottery for noble purposes and some for common use?"

&

IF WE ARE CONVINCED OF BEING "A GOD ORIGINAL," WE WILL NOT QUIBBLE OVER THE DESIGN.

Pruning Trees and Trimming Shrubbery

JOB 5:7

"Yet man is born to trouble as surely as sparks fly upward."

There are many ways of relieving tension. My husband trims trees or bushes. It's possible to tell what psychological state he's in by checking our shrubbery. One stress-filled day he came home early and attacked our white birch tree. He not only pruned away branches, he actually sawed off limbs. However, realizing he might have gotten carried away, he was less brutal on the smaller trees. Had his mood persisted, our shrubs could have become prematurely bald.

Year after year weeds had taken over our vegetable "garden" along the back of the house. We added 20 more shrubs, which now completely surround our dwelling. This eliminated my suffocated vegetables and also provided Walt with extra therapy. It is fortunate he has found such a creative outlet.

Scores of books on tension, anxiety, depression, anger, and worry line bookstore shelves. However, pruning trees or trimming shrubbery may be more beneficial than a book.

እ⁀

TRIMMING SHRUBS AND READING BOOKS HELP, BUT THIS VERSE FROM MATTHEW HAS THE ANSWERS.

MATTHEW 6:34

"Therefore do not worry about tomorrow, for tomorrow will worry about itself. Each day has enough trouble of its own."

113

The Lord Is Our Shepherd

PSALM 65:13

"The meadows are covered with flocks and the valleys are mantled with grain; they shout for joy and sing."

Lambs are a sign of spring. When we see pictures of spring, there are usually lambs scampering about in a green meadow, dotted with flowers. We raised sheep on our farm. Ewes are not very hearty creatures, and it was not uncommon to lose a ewe when the lambs were born. More than one lamb was raised on a bottle in my grandparents' cellar. One lamb we raised became a pet. However, later it turned on us and became dangerous. We were spared the agony of getting rid of it—the lamb died of pneumonia.

It was an exciting day when the sheep were sheared. After clipping the wool and bagging it, the sheep look naked as they were freed and left to run. If the weather had already turned warm, it was a relief to see them stripped of their heavy coat, no longer panting. In the Old Testament, sheepshearing time was a festive occasion.

The Lord is our shepherd; we are the sheep. Any knowledge about sheep we may glean is helpful in understanding our own condition.

ISAIAH 40:11

"He tends his flock like a shepherd: He gathers the lambs in his arms and carries them close to his heart; he gently leads those that have young."

❧

BUT KNOWLEDGE OF THE SHEPHERD IS EVEN MORE IMPORTANT.

114

Linford and Ada

MATTHEW 9:37

"Then he said to his disciples, 'The harvest is plentiful but the workers are few.' "

PSALM 34:8

"O taste and see that the Lord is good: blessed is the man who trusteth in him" (KJV).

Ever since I have known my husband, his oldest brother Linford and wife Ada were in mission work in the Northwest. They wore out many cars driving folks to Sunday school and preaching at mission churches in Minnesota and Canada. Peace River, Slave Lake, the Yukon, Alaska—these were places Linford wrote about in his letters. His Northwoods stories kept children and adults on the edge of their seats. He had the rare ability of meeting unusual people however he traveled. If journals and diaries tell stories, I know his do.

When we heard of his death, I thought of the obituary the Edmonton paper would print. But obituaries are cold facts—age, wife, place of birth, parents, children, membership in organizations, and church affiliation. It would not include that his call to the "harvest" in the West came before they were married. Nor would it tell of the three-month honeymoon through the same area where he later preached. Nor of his solo trip in a Piper Cub from Pennsylvania to the edge of the Canadian Rockies.

If all the lives Linford touched in his 76 years were gathered at one place, they would fill a stadium. And always there supporting him was Ada—even to his last breath.

❧

PSALM 34:8 WAS LINFORD'S FAVORITE VERSE, AND THE REFERENCE APPEARED ON THE ENVELOPE OF HIS WEEKLY LETTER TO HIS PARENTS.

My Rainbow-Colored Dish

MATTHEW 6:19

"Do not store up for yourselves treasures on earth, where moth and rust destroy, and where thieves break in and steal."

I have a dark carnival glass dish. I used it for mints until my uncle told me of its approximate worth. Now the rainbow-colored dish is in the cupboard with the door closed. No one sees it; no one enjoys it. It rests there accumulating more years and more value.

Before I knew of its worth, I washed it in the dishwasher. Each time it came out more beautiful. There was something about the agitation that seemed to free the irridescent colors.

Breaking dishes comes natural to me. I broke dishes my mother had for years. We bought the set of china used by my husband's parents beyond their golden anniversary. I broke more pieces in a few years than they did in 50.

But what is the sense of storing the dish? If I keep it hidden for another 25 years and it's sold for several hundred dollars, what good will it have accomplished?

I'm going to use it! This versicolor treasure will again cradle mints.

LUKE 9:24-25

"For whoever wants to save his life will lose it, but whoever loses his life for me will save it. What good is it for a man to gain the whole world, and yet lose or forfeit his very self?"

❧

IT IS MUCH BETTER TO BE BROKEN WHILE BEING USEFUL.

116

The Influence of Books

JOHN 21:25

"Jesus did many other things as well. If every one of them were written down, I suppose that even the whole world would not have room for the books that would be written."

I have a love affair with books—to a point. A cobbler's children may go barefooted, but this bookstore family is never without books. We receive books in the mail and bring books home from the store. Every summer we add more to our collection after the Christian Booksellers Convention. One day I informed my husband we also had to live in our house, not just keep books.

One Wednesday, our day off, we started to clean house on our bookshelves. It was a wise decision to have my husband help me. His involvement opened his eyes to my problem. A good supply of empty boxes were soon filled. Some old Christian fiction was saved for the children. Other books were given to our church library. My husband had a "free" garage sale in our store basement, and the rest were thrown away. Seeing all the books that were left, I wondered where we had kept the many books we got rid of—and we hadn't even touched the 16 bookshelves in the basement!

The Bible records a public "book-burning"—the result of believing in Christ. It must have been quite a sight!

ACTS 19:19

"A number who had practiced sorcery brought their scrolls together and burned them publicly. When they calculated the value of the scrolls, the total came to fifty thousand drachmas."

ॐ

WE CANNOT MEASURE THE INFLUENCE OF BOOKS—GOOD OR BAD.

117

Pulling Mustard

MARK 4:31-32

"It is like a mustard seed, which is the smallest seed you plant in the ground. Yet when planted it grows and becomes the largest of all garden plants, with such big branches that the birds of the air can perch in its shade."

MATTHEW 17:20

"Because you have so little faith, I tell you the truth, if you have faith as small as a grain of mustard seed, you can say to the mountain, 'Move from here to there' and it will move. Nothing will be impossible for you."

Before the days of weed killers, we were sent to the fields to pull mustard out by the roots. Some plants were so sturdy that birds built nests in them. I remember how shocked I was to see some city folks carefully digging mustard, making sure some ground remained on the roots for transplanting in their city garden. To this day I see no beauty in mustard, even though I realize if you would take yellow mustard flowers, large purple clover, some white Queen Anne's Lace, and a few meadow daisies, the bouquet could be sent F.T.D.

I did not consider my trip to the field to pull mustard a field trip. It was not a fun day. Occasionally mustard stalks were so well-rooted that when they finally loosened up, I would lose my balance and fall to the ground. The stuff left my hands stained green, horrible green!

I was not thinking of Christ's unusual object lesson of the mustard seed. I wonder if Jesus had to pull mustard when he was young, since reference to a mustard seed is his alone. He was certainly familiar with it.

INFERRING THAT OUR FAITH IS LESS THAN THE SIZE OF A MUSTARD SEED SHOULD SET US THINKING.

118

We Live by a Name

PROVERBS 22:1

"A good name is more desirable than great riches; to be esteemed is better than silver or gold."

I remember dreaming of names for a baby before I was married. If we thought about marriage we thought about children. Children came with marriage. And children needed names.

It was common in my generation to have a name repeated in a family. I had two cousins named Sam, named after my grandfather. I also had a cousin Ruth. If the last name was not used as identification, we could say, "Phares's Ruth" or "Norman's Sam."

We live by a name. We die by a name. We are remembered by name. However, our name and personality "homogenize" until they cannot be separated. We seldom think of friends' names without thinking of their character, disposition, temperament—their whole personality. We remain strangers to people who only know us by name.

2 PETER 1:5-7

"For this very reason, make every effort to add to your faith goodness; and to goodness, knowledge; and to knowledge, self-control; and to self-control, perseverance; and to perseverance, godliness; and to godliness, brotherly kindness; and to brotherly kindness, love."

≈

EVEN AN UNDESIRABLE NAME COULD BE RESTORED TO DIGNITY BY FOLLOWING THIS LIST IN 2 PETER.

Are Your Doors Locked?

The only time my parents locked their kitchen door was when they went on a trip. Our door was open night and day, whether we were home or not. Can you imagine such freedom? There was no concern about finding the key, no worry when you crawled into bed, wondering if the door was safely locked.

After checking the doors at our house, I drag into bed. My husband settles in bed too and promptly asks, "Did you lock the door?" With uncertainty I reply, "I think so." Disgruntled, he gets out of bed and checks both doors again. The need to have the doors locked becomes an obsession.

Today we have burglar alarms, double locks, protective chains, and still don't feel safe. For one week I wish we could ignore the locks, carelessly push the doors shut, and rest in peaceful assurance that all is well.

CHRIST ALWAYS ADDS ANOTHER DIMENSION.

120

Revealing Albums

1 CORINTHIANS 13:17

"When I was a child, I thought like a child, I reasoned like a child. When I became a man, I put childish ways behind me."

There's no way to keep a family album up-to-date. We are changing all the time—from the day we are born till the day we die. If the hair is cut shorter or left to grow longer, the photograph is compared to the present look. How quickly we have put away the graduation pictures to make room for our children's wedding pictures. The yearly school pictures of the grandchildren are being added to the gallery.

On the first photograph I received of my husband he had so much hair he actually had it thinned. Now on his trip to the barber, he declares he has to have his hairs counted. As for my "Sweet 16" picture—you would never recognize me.

Physical growth comes naturally. Mentally we have learned to talk, think, and reason like a child. Spiritually we may be wavering about "putting childish ways behind us."

❧

1 CORINTHIANS 14:20

"Brothers, stop thinking like children. In regard to evil be infants, but in your thinking be adults."

WHAT A REVEALING ALBUM THAT WOULD MAKE—ONE FILLED WITH PICTURES OF OUR SPIRITUAL PROGRESS!

Enjoy Who You Are

EPHESIANS 1:4

"For he chose us in him before the creation of the world to be holy and blameless in his sight."

It took Alex Haley 10 years and a half million miles of travel to gather the information for his book, *Roots*. He did what he felt he had to do.

However, I don't believe all of us should follow Haley's zeal to track our ancestry back to our roots. Why should the rest of us feel our pedigree is so important? Need I have a guilt complex if I lack the desire to visit the exact spot in Germany where my family tree took root? What if I had been a doorstep baby with no way of tracing my roots? It should not affect my being a productive person. Probing into our lineage could be disappointing as well as fulfilling.

Unless "who you came from" and "where you came from" are driving passions, I suggest you enjoy who you are.

EPHESIANS 1:5

"In love he predestined us to be adopted as his sons through Jesus Christ, in accordance with his pleasure and will."

ॐ

IN THE FAMILY OF GOD, WE ARE ALL ADOPTED.

I Was Never More Sincere

MATTHEW 7:21

"Not everyone who says to me 'Lord, Lord' will enter the kingdom of heaven, but only he who does the will of my Father who is in heaven."

The tile on our bathroom floor looked grubby. I measured the floor, went to a local department store, and bought a washable rug. I took my best scissors and followed the instructions. I worked for two hours, fitting the rug to our bathroom floor. Clippings of yarn were under the rug and on top of the rug. After sweeping the fuzz and looking at my project, I was pleased.

After three years of washing, the rubber backing of my beige rug became brittle. I decided my bathroom needed some excitement, so I purchased one in coral pink. This time I attacked the job with full assurance, since I could use the old one for a pattern. With well-thought-out logic, I laid rubber against rubber, so it wouldn't slip. I went cutting blissfully around the old rug into the new coral tuft. It never occurred to me till I had finished snipping that I was in for trouble. I could not believe what I had done! The rug would only fit upside down.

If being sincere is important, that rug would have come out perfect. I was never more sincere. But I was wrong—dead wrong.

JOHN 3:5

"I tell you the truth, unless a man is born of water and the Spirit, he cannot enter the kingdom of God."

ᛞ

Jesus Is the Only Way.

123

Not Every Traffic Light Is Green

JAMES 1:2-3

"Consider it pure joy, my brothers, whenever you face trials of many kinds, because you know that the testing of your faith develops perseverance."

Waiting should be easy—in a doctor's office, a traffic jam, or for a business appointment. It may be the free time you've been looking for. You don't have to do anything, just sit and relax. However, the elevation in blood pressure and the increased adrenalin charging through your body when you are forced to wait create all kinds of problems. Tempers flare, and uncontrollable restlessness ruins what could be a pleasurable diversion.

Is there ever a day when we don't have to wait somewhere? Not every traffic light we approach is green. Even with computer registers, grocery lines don't move fast enough. Looking for a quick getaway, we search for the fastest moving lane.

If we don't take advantage of these rest periods, they will exhaust us. How can we make these "waits" productive? How can we endure them gracefully? Seldom is our extreme haste justified.

ءب

IF YOU WANT TO PASS THE TEST IN PATIENCE, A TRAFFIC JAM IS WORTH QUITE A FEW CREDIT HOURS.

JAMES 1:4

"Perseverance must finish its work so that you may be mature and complete, not lacking anything."

Seasons Take Turns

Before the days of air conditioning, our only choice was to live with the season, not control it. There wasn't a cool place to go. Fortunate was the family who had a summer kitchen or spring house. We had a small underground "cave" in our backyard for the storing of perishables. Since many houses were made of stone, we were protected for several days from the scorching heat. However, the upstairs and attic absorbed the heat quicker. We slept with our heads at the foot of the bed, trying to catch a breeze.

During harvest time the men wore cotton caps and tied red hankies around their necks. The perspiration on their faces attracted the black dust until their faces were hardly recognizable.

As for swimming, we went to the creek, where the cows preceeded and succeeded us. Leeches were a constant source of irritation. "Snake doctors" skimmed in and out amongst the bathers. Even the kids from town walked to these rural "beaches." It is a wonder we didn't get sick from the polluted waters. Our interest was in being cool, even in the heat of summer.

෨

GOD PROMISED NOAH THE SEASONS WOULD ALWAYS TAKE TURNS—A STABILITY WE CAN COUNT ON.

A Matter of Life or Death

1 CORINTHIANS 9:24

"Do you know that in a race all runners run, but only one gets the prize? Run in such a way as to get the prize."

We have an ongoing debate at our house about exercise—especially walking. I do not enjoy aimless walking. I contend my body doesn't care if I use my muscles to scrub floors or walk around the block. In our store we are going up and down steps all day. Does my coronary system reject this movement as nothing? (My excuses are flimsy.)

Olympic athletes, however, cannot do what they feel like doing. They train to win. They eat to win. They actually live to win. The runners, swimmers, gymnasts, and contestants in all categories reveal how much "punishment" the human body can take. Winning is a consuming passion. Only another runner knows what discipline is involved to win a 26-mile race. Years of work precede the prize.

1 CORINTHIANS 9:25

"Everyone who competes in the games goes into strict training. They do it to get a crown that will not last; but we do it to get a crown that will last forever."

❧

IN THE CHRISTIAN RACE THE CROWN IS ETERNAL. WE CANNOT AFFORD TO BE APATHETIC.

126